The

Silent Mentor

Sylvia Mayall

2QT Limited (Publishing)

First Edition Published 2011
2QT Limited (Publishing)
Burton In Kendal
Cumbria LA6 1NJ
www.2qt.co.uk

Cover Image painted by
Vincent Vesty

Cover Typeset/Design
Dale Rennard

Printed in Great Britain

A CIP catalogue record for this book is available
from the British Library
ISBN 978-1-908098-18-4

Acknowledgements

Ingleton Library, Ingleton, North Yorkshire.

Campcraft, Bolton, Lancashire.

Holyrood Church, Swinton, Lancashire.

St Cuthbert's Centre, Holy Island, Northumbria.

Dalesbridge, Austwick, Nr Settle, North Yorkshire.

Glenfinnan Dining Car, Glenfinnan Railway Museum, Glenfinnan Inverness-shire.

Cannich Camping, Strathglass, Inverness-shire.

L.A.D.'s, Caol, Inverness-shire.

Clapham Village Store, Clapham, North Yorkshire.

White Scar Cave, Nr.Ingleton, North Yorkshire.

The Fishermen's Mission Mallaig, Mallaig, Scotland.

Dyffryn Farm, Powys, Wales

Royal Bank of Scotland.

Creation Gardens, Nantmel, Wales.

Our Lady of Hyning Monastery, Warton, Nr Carnforth Lancashire

Settle Methodist Church, Settle, North Yorkshire.

The Automobile Association.

And of course to Avylis's friend...

For Mum,
who led me to the path,

and

Carol,
who enabled me to travel on...

Chapter One

I'd followed the instructions precisely, but the bracken, thistles and fledgling trees had claimed the narrow track, and scraped against the undercarriage of the car. My destination lay three miles ahead, it was getting dark, I was in unknown territory and this wasn't the time or place to refine my skills at reversing in order to extricate myself. I pulled up. After pacing slowly along the track for about a mile, searching for any unseen hazards, I turned back, reassured that the track was passable with care, and coaxed the car forward.

The small stone building emerged amidst the trees and on reaching it I released a huge sigh of relief, not just because I'd reached my destination, but at the sight of sufficient ground to execute a three-point turn.

The gate, hanging on one hinge, stood in knee high growth, so I climbed over the broken wire fence. Two grey milky eyes, set under a rusty corrugated iron brow, home to a small central chimney stared back at me. The rough, ill-fitting wooden door was secured with a padlock. I took the key from the envelope, fitted it in the rusty lock and turned it firmly; then pushed the door cautiously, like a trespasser with a conscience.

My eyes adjusted to the darkness. There was a lamp, hanging from the low ceiling. I tapped it gently, heard the swish of liquid, and unhooked it. A brief examination revealed that it had a new wick, primed and ready for use; even so, would it light after being neglected for so long? I found a box of matches by the hearth, and after several failed attempts to strike one, only to see the tips fly off, I struck three together and a flame hissed into life.

The lamp threw fitful shadows across the irregular grey stones that made up the walls; a bare wooden table and chair in the corner; and a cast iron pot hung over the ready set grate, with kindling and logs neatly piled at one side. To the other side of the grate stood a saw, axe, poker and metal bucket, and above, a rack fixed to the ceiling on a simple rope pulley. I was standing on a threadbare mat that covered the flagged floor, with my hand resting on a low backed chair.

Through a gap in the wall I found myself in a smaller area with a crude wooden shelf supporting an enamel bowl and jug. A missing brick above the shelf provided no light as dusk had descended.

As I walked back through the gap my foot caught on a thin mattress; at one end was a neat bundle of threadbare clothes, at the other end a rolled blanket. Apart from the cobwebs, considering the place had been empty for several years it was reasonably clean; in fact it looked as if the occupant might return at any time. Removing the dusty rug thrown over the low chair, I sat on the thin cushion watching the shadows twitch erratically round the walls.

~ ~ ~

This, I thought, was the abode of an elderly man, content with the little he had. A recluse who managed without all the material possessions others took for granted, yet treasuring the things that he had, and apparently had all he needed. He would have cooked on his open fire, where he must have heated water for washing both himself and his clothes. There was the stream outside for water and the wooded area for fuel. Yet there were no cups, plates, pans or utensils of any kind, surely even a recluse needed the basics. I dismissed the thought that anything had been removed, as it was an isolated bothy and the security – such as it was - had not been tampered with, and in any case the place was so tidy. The only people who may be able to answer the questions, filing themselves rapidly in my brain, were the villagers; but how much they would reveal to a stranger remained to be seen. The light from the lamp hesitated and died, it was getting late, yet I had no wish to move.

~ ~ ~

Leaving the bothy I replaced the padlock and returned to the car. I ignored the bed and breakfast sign in favour of the small hotel twenty miles away, which would be anonymous, not wanting to become involved in polite conversation, not tonight.

Chapter Two

I woke early, ate the continental breakfast left outside the bedroom door, and departed. The announcer on the car radio informed me it was eight twenty-seven.

~ ~ ~

Just twenty four hours ago I'd driven off the ferry from the Outer Hebrides where I'd been wild camping, and seen the notice bearing my name, held across the chest of a tall, slender man, maybe sixty or thereabouts. His well fitting charcoal slacks, navy jacket, pale blue shirt and dark tie were immaculate; he looked like a mannequin who had escaped from the window of a bespoke tailor. I pulled over and opened the door as he walked towards me.

"Frank Hodgson," he announced quietly, with a smile usually reserved for greeting a long lost relative or friend, and doffed his cap. I took the card he offered and read:

Hodgson and Wilson
Solicitors

"Could you spare a moment please?" he requested, "it is important. Maybe we could have a coffee?" he suggested, looking towards the small café on the quayside. I nodded and followed his easy stride.

He opened the door for me, and once inside indicated a table near the window, suggesting that we may as well enjoy the view; it was also the table farthest away from the counter. I walked across to the table leaving Mr. Hodgson to order the drinks. In different circumstances I may have had reason to be cautious, but this quietly spoken gentleman could never be perceived as a threat – could he? The solicitor walked over to join me setting a tray on the table, and carefully placing a mug of coffee in front of me, before removing his hat to reveal short grey hair with a precise parting, and sat down.

"It is just a formality," he said, "but do you have any identification with you?" I produced my driving licence, which he immediately handed back. He clearly knew who I was, so I waited for his explanation.

"I have to inform you," he began, "that you are the sole beneficiary of a legacy, and my firm is acting as sole executor for your benefactor, Avylis." He paused and looked at me with questioning dark brown eyes and the hint of a smile.

"I am sorry Mr. Hodgson, I don't know anyone by that name, there is obviously some mistake." Was this the reaction that he had expected, for he showed no surprise?

"Please allow me to explain," he said.

Explain what? I thought, as the solicitor began to speak.

"According to my instructions it is my duty to undertake two tasks; firstly to deliver an envelope *personally* into your hand, and secondly to secure the..." for a second his easy articulation deserted him, "property, which was done almost immediately. Fortunately my friend, in the area on holiday, was able to arrange it. We are a small practice based in Dorset, just about as far away as we could be from the Highlands—" I interrupted him as he may later regret divulging his information to the wrong person.

"But, who... why? This must be a mist—" I insisted, but the solicitor silenced me gently lifting one finger up.

"I can assure you that there is no mistake. You will appreciate we have had more than enough time to check and recheck all the details during the three years it has taken to trace you."

That was certainly true; he would not have found me easily. There was nothing to say, I just gazed into deep calm pools of treacle, twinkling in the reflected light, lips on the verge of a smile and an immaculate knotted tie, as my mind tried to assimilate the news it had just received.

His voice was both appealing and apologetic when he spoke.

"Please believe me," he started, "I know you must have many questions and I'm not being reticent, I genuinely cannot help you. The answers, I am afraid, you will have to find for yourself, but maybe this will help." He drew a small envelope from his inside pocket. "I sincerely hope so." His features now matched the seriousness in his voice as our eyes met for a few moments, and then with great reverence, as if he were entrusting me with a Holy Relic, he leaned forward, and placing the envelope in my hand, said, "For there is nothing else."

As our hands parted, he sat back, inhaled deeply and sighed quietly, but the tension in his body was evident. Could it be that he was relieved of his duty towards my benefactor, yet somehow concerned for the new owner, now in possession of the envelope? Had I, in my confusion, given him reason to believe I was fearful? Perhaps, because his genial smile appeared on cue, as if to reassure me, as he joked, "My only hope is that it does not take you half the time and effort to find the answers that was beholden on me to trace you. Thank you for your time and I wish you well, I really do."

The last three words were spoken slowly, stressed with sincerity. What was going on?

"I don't know much about legacies," I admitted, "but is it usual for anything to have to be handed over personally by a solicitor?"

"No," he replied, "you're quite right, but I must abide by my client's wishes in the matter." I waited but he wasn't about to expound further. The conversation was over and it was time to leave. I thanked him for the coffee, and apologised for causing him so much trouble.

"Oh, please don't apologise, I had a legitimate excuse to drive through the glorious countryside and stay away from the office for a couple of nights. It is I who should really be thanking you. However, I have now fulfilled the requirements of the legacy and my duty is completed."

"It has been my privilege to meet you," he said as we stood

outside by my car and shook hands. He looked towards his car and then turned back "Please, would you mind contacting me, the numbers on the card, when, that is, if you leave the property?" I nodded, but was left with the undeniable feeling that Mr. Hodgson had left without asking of me the one question he would have dearly liked answered, simply because I believed he would have deemed it an intrusion, and Mr. Hodgson was far too professional to overstep the mark; but what would that question have been?

Once inside my car I fingered the small plain envelope, turning it over several times looking at the plain white paper, before running my finger under the seal to open it. My benefactor had left me a roughly drawn map, but with precise instructions on it, and a small key - to open what - a case, or a locker?

~ ~ ~

And here I was twenty-four hours later driving back to my newly acquired property, past the village stores, the 'Buck Inn', a single storey community hall, the playground of the junior school, and the 'Singing Kettle' café; all strung together along the narrow lane by stone cottages. The lane had no reason to travel any further and simply blended into the countryside around and beyond.

Entering the bothy I still felt like a trespasser. How could I disturb, rummage through, a stranger's private life? I had no right. It was only when looking around in daylight, that I saw there were no drawers, no cupboards, nowhere to enclose anything, all was in view. There was nothing else to see. Maybe it would be better to lock up and leave; maybe that was the answer. Whoever had lived here, perhaps I should leave their memories at peace. But why should anyone leave me nothing? And who was Avylis?

As I went to get the blanket from the mattress, to place on the chair which was bone hard, I was distracted by a sudden deluge of rain and wandered over to the window, but it was too dark to see anything. Returning to the mattress I spotted a fragment of paper, caught in the light of the flickering lamp, on top of the clothes on the bed and gently pulled it out of the shirt pocket. I unfolded it and read:

> *My heart has at once been seared and calmed; wounds open and raw have been soothed the instant you spoke. You fanned the flames of that love, and then smothered them with ignorance. Your love rose like the sun at dawn, only to be eclipsed at noon. You nurtured me as a young shoot, and then cruelly uprooted me.*
>
> *I never stopped loving you; because one day you will claim me for your own; not because of your fickle love for me, but rather my enduring love for you. We will be one, as it was always meant to be.*

Had he written it and then never sent it; or was he the recipient? Yet somebody content to live with so little surely was not capable of such torment. Maybe he had become a recluse because of unrequited love for someone who flashed in and out of his life, always leaving him bereft. Yet he had found reason to hope. Had his lover known the anguish, hurt and hope he had lived with? Had she deliberately taunted him; was she just fickle or had he himself been too patient, not wanting to coerce her in any way, knowing she had to come willingly to a love freely given?

For, it would seem, all he had to offer was his love, and that had to be enough.

Chapter Three

I paid for a coffee in The Singing Kettle café and sat at the corner table. A short, elderly man, stooping badly, entered and I wondered how much pain was he in. He removed his hat, raised his eyes and greeted me as he sat at the table opposite and was served his drink immediately. He chatted to me about the weather, answering his own questions. When he turned his attention to his coffee I suggested that he may be able to help me, and asked if he knew who had lived in the bothy. The man studied his coffee, and then looked at me carefully, consideration rather than irritation on his face, before inviting me to sit with him.

"Oh, it has been empty now, let me see, it must be three years maybe more. We never knew who lived there, we saw her occ..." The next words I missed.

"I'm sorry; you were saying you saw her?" I said.

The man repeated himself.

"She came to the shop every two weeks, always bought the same items. She handed over the money and Mrs. Bea changed it for the same amount. You see she dropped her change once and I picked it up for her. That fiver stretched to infinity," he chuckled softly to himself.

"You know you're the first person I've ever told. One look from Mrs. Bea at the time ensured that, you didn't tell, she has a heart of gold.

Mrs. Bea knew, we all knew, the lady was poor, had nothing, and yet she was always smiling as she listened to other people. She brought a sort of... peace. Yes peace, difficult to explain, but the days she came to the village everything seemed somewhat calmer.

"Do you know what I mean?"

"Yes, I believe I do," I replied, "she sounds like a very special lady, and please don't worry, your secret's safe with me." His breakfast was served and I stood to leave as he rose slowly and painfully. We shook hands as I thanked him.

~ ~ ~

The young lady at the village shop informed me that, "Mrs. Bea eventually retired three years ago when..." but had quickly checked herself in response to the look of another customer and went on to explain that Mrs. Bea lived at 'Gazania Cottage', the one with the yellow door.

There was one place left in the village where I might find some answers, the 'Buck Inn'. It was nearly midday, so I could have some lunch and maybe find out a little more; being quite aware that as a stranger asking questions in a small village, I could easily alienate myself. There was little time left to find out as much as possible. By tomorrow everything could change to mere politeness and ignorance of even who their next door neighbours were, and who could blame them.

The owner of the 'Buck Inn', a solid man, dressed in corduroys and a Welsh rugby shirt, greeted me cheerfully as he reached for an empty beer bottle on the counter with such a huge hand that I stiffened, convinced it would shatter in his grip. He turned, bent down and gently placed it in a container behind the bar. In the few seconds before he turned to face me, my ears had tuned into the right wavelength, and I received the answer to my question, in a broad Yorkshire dialect.

He informed me that the bothy was already empty when he bought the inn and moved into the village. Rumours abounded, some said the owner would be back, others that the land was in disputed ownership, and, if he was honest, villagers were suspicious of incomers. (The last remark was matter-of-fact; he was merely making an observation, considering himself to be a villager.) However, what he was certain about was that two visitors

14

had enquired who owned it, and about buying, renovating and extending the property, but permission had been refused; permission to run mains to the land had also been refused. Those people had stayed at the inn on several occasions but had finally given up trying to untangle the details. There had been no enquiries for over two years to his knowledge.

I thanked the landlord with the Yorkshire dialect – who supported the Welsh rugby team – and now considered himself a Scot, with a Lancashire accent, and ordered a coffee.

Chapter Four

Mrs. Bea, a short, elderly lady, had neat wavy silver hair, a clear complexion and rosy cheeks. She invited me in, wiping floured hands on an apron spread across her well-nourished figure, to the delicious aromas of vanilla and bread. We were soon seated with tea and homemade cakes in front of her log fire.

"Now what can I do for you, my dear?" Mrs. Bea said, as she leaned forward looking directly at me with blue eyes edged with laughter lines, and what was surely a permanent smile.

"I wonder if you could tell me who lived in the bothy down the track?"

"Ah," Mrs. Bea turned to gaze at the fire for a moment and then turned back to engage me.

"Yes indeed I miss her. I think we all miss her in our own way," she said reminiscing.

"Miss her?" I queried.

"Yes, three years ago we thought she'd left. We didn't see her for several weeks, then one day she came in for her shopping. I had of course put her shopping to one side." Mrs. Bea looked at the fire and itemised the shopping list, as I speculated it may be to convince herself she hadn't forgotten, or for the memories it evoked, and hoped those memories were not too painful.

"I will never forget that day," she continued, "she looked thinner, yet somehow stronger, difficult to explain really. But that was the last time we saw her." Mrs Bea paused to sip her tea. That was the second time today I had heard that phrase, 'difficult to explain'. Mrs. Bea, holding the cup in both hands, resting it on her knee continued her story. "She never spoke, not a word. I often wondered if she was mute, but she wasn't deaf. Do you know she always smiled as if she hadn't a care in the world, and yet she had nothing? I suppose she could easily be mistaken for a tramp, and yet I never thought of her like that. Everybody accepted her. She was regarded as one of the villagers, and that in itself was amazing. I am afraid, my dear, that country folk are not always welcoming to incomers; yet for some reason the villagers liked her, in fact I would go so far as to say they loved her, and not out of pity, no not that." She sat forward. "Now will you have another cup of tea, my dear?" My cup was already being filled. "And please help yourself to another scone," she said, gently nudging the plate towards me. "Don't be shy now there's plenty more." She settled back in her chair and we sat in silence, sipping tea and nibbling scones.

"I remember, Charlie," I turned to face Mrs Bea, as she continued, "tearaway youngster he was. It was shortly after the lady arrived. He rode his bicycle straight into her, never watched where he was going," she sighed. "Knocked her against the wall, it must have hurt her. She went over to the boy, helped him up and then took his head gently between her hands, looked at him for a second, then picked up his bicycle and wheeled it to him. The whole incident was over in a flash. But do you know what was the truly amazing thing about it, my dear?" I shook my head. "The amazing thing was, his mother, always belting the boy for something or another, just stood and watched. We all did. Charlie rode off on his bicycle waving at the lady. After that people would stop and talk to her. She always looked directly at them, listened, and Gilbert used to say, she answered with her eyes."

"Gilbert?"

"Gilbert, now there's an extraordinary man, my dear. I do not always sleep very well, and I used to see him at six, sometimes earlier peddling on that old bicycle of his with a box balanced precariously on the little rack at the back, and a rucksack on his back, looking round careful not to be seen. Always wondered why? Now you understand I am not normally inquisitive, but everyone knew that he suffered greatly with his back, so why did he do it? Anyway, I was concerned that he would harm his back even more and wondered if I should have a word with him, but it is so difficult, I wouldn't have wanted him to think I was spying on him. Then one morning I saw something fall from his bicycle, and went to pick it up, and the mystery was solved; he was taking logs for the lady, he wouldn't want her to be cold." Then Mrs. Bea answered my question without the need of the asking. "But where she came from, who she was, where she went, we can never know. But I doubt many will forget her." She bent forward, refilled the tea cups and poked the fire before placing another log in the grate, while I enquired how Gilbert was. Mrs. Bea sat back in her chair.

"Oh, he manages, my dear, he is slower now but still mentally alert. He spends most mornings at the café reading the paper and doing the crossword. I used to pop in until recently. He always has his breakfast there. I remember once, tourists came in and when he left, one of them went over to Eileen." Mrs. Bea answered my puzzled look. "Eileen runs the café. Thin as a rake," she added, "anyway," she said returning to her theme, "on this day the visitor went over to say the old man had left without paying his bill. Eileen just told them he paid when he came in." Mrs. Bea stopped talking, shook her head and sighed. She didn't need to add, 'if only visitors didn't try to inform us on how we ought to handle matters'.

"Truth is, my dear," Mrs. Bea explained, "Eileen refuses to let him pay, has done for years. I only know because when I was in once, Gilbert went to pay and Eileen whispered, 'Be off with you.' Good soul she is but quiet with it, wouldn't want the world to know."

"Gilbert? Would he have a rounded face, deep brown eyes, thick grey hair?" I asked.

"Yes, my dear. You've met him then?"

"He was at the café earlier - as you said - having breakfast and reading his paper."

"Yes that would be Gilbert," she confirmed.

I thanked Mrs. Bea for her hospitality, delicious cakes and her help.

On opening the gate I turned to Mrs. Bea and saw for the first time a sadness in her eyes.

"It wasn't that we didn't care," she said, "most of the villagers wanted to help, and would have, but she seemed to want to be alone and we didn't want to intrude, so there was nothing we could do."

I looked at this gentle, loving lady, before answering, "Oh, I wouldn't say that. It seems to me that she found shelter here for a while, and the villagers not only welcomed her but between them provided all her needs, small as they may have been, in a loving, generous and unobtrusive way. You said few of the villagers would forget her, likewise I doubt very much if she will forget the villagers." I waved as I drove off, and watched Mrs. Bea waving through the rear view mirror, until she was out of sight.

Chapter Five

Why had I assumed a man had lived at the bothy? How could anyone live in the place for two years? It was after all, just a shelter with no amenities, not even a sink, toilet or any form of cooking equipment, lit by a single oil lamp; and yet I'd sat here last night with no wish to move, and according to the villagers, despite her poverty Avylis appeared content. But if she only went into the village every two weeks, what did she do between the visits; where did she go; and did she have any visitors that the villagers were unaware of?

Mr. Hodgson's words echoed in my brain, not for the first time, 'The answers, I'm afraid; you will have to find for yourself.'

Why should anyone go to the trouble of making a will to leave a stranger nothing, and why me? Exactly! I thought, why me? My name was not chosen at random, so whoever Avylis was she must have at least known of me, it doesn't necessarily follow that I would know her; yet there must be some connection; but finding that would be like searching for the proverbial needle in a haystack. There must be some clue, apart from the piece of cryptic writing I had found in the shirt pocket.

~ ~ ~

Having had another look there was nothing else wrapped in the pitiful pile of clothing on the mattress, except cutlery for one, a tin, mug and plate. Under the blanket was a small leather suitcase. What was this?

It was the only object that had to be opened to discover its contents there was no other possible place to 'hide' anything. I looked at it - not sure of what I should do. It might contain private possessions, and if so, it was surely all that this person had retained at the end of her life. There must be someone, somewhere who should have them, who would cherish them; someone to whom they would mean something, for they would mean nothing at all to me. Looking closer I could see there was no form of lock on it. Somebody, with so few possessions surely hadn't simply forgotten to take it; and why attempt to hide it, such a useless ploy in the circumstances. Did it contain any form of identification? If so I may be able to return it to a relative or friend, but surely the solicitor would have known; why hadn't he sorted it out? Should I phone him? I knew that would be useless. If it was to be returned to anybody I had no option but to open it to see if there was some identification.

The case was full of note pads and numerous loose sheets of paper. Then I remembered, amongst her shopping, Mrs. Bea had mentioned there was always an exercise book or notepad and pen. She had said that the villagers had speculated she might have written letters, if she could write, yet no one had ever seen her post one; neither had she bought any stamps. So had she spent her time writing, but what and why? I could find nothing else in the main room so went into the smaller one. Here apart from the wooden shelf, basin and jug, there was on the opposite wall a small slate slop stone and a bar of soap, probably missed either in the dim light of last night or as a result of my stumbling over the mattress. Underneath was a bottle of oil, from behind which scuttled a field mouse. There was also a small low door; as I drew the bolt I could only assume that there was a perfectly logical explanation for why a space no more than twenty feet by eight should warrant two entrances, maybe it was where hay was stored for sheep or cattle, no longer here.

Outside the back door, against the wall, was a small neat stack of logs. The stream was splashing recklessly over boulders, trees reached up towards a light grey sky, with pools of blue and flashes of white; mountains soared into a purple mist and pierced the very heavens themselves. The scene was one of unshackled beauty, left to wander wherever it chose. I stood at complete peace.

~ ~ ~

Back inside, sitting on the mattress, I looked through the paperwork. Amongst several reporters' pads, there were also numerous loose sheets, all hand written. Maybe here I would find a clue; but having already decided my course of action there was nothing more to be done until the morning so I placed the papers back under the blanket and returned to the hotel.

Chapter Six

I called in the local store near the hotel to pick up food, cleaning materials, coal and oil, before leaving to drive back to the bothy; not wanting to be seen by my 'neighbours' buying these items, for curiosity would, sooner rather than later, be aroused as to my daily activities. Country folk, I knew, would speculate on a stranger's presence, and as I had to-date not divulged anything, but rather, had asked questions of them, time was running out. If I was not to leave soon then some explanation would be required. The water in the cauldron over the fire had heated, so I cleaned the windows, scrubbed the table top, swept and mopped the floor and wiped the glass chimney on the oil lamp. It was while I was scrubbing the hot irons in front of the fire, (rather foolishly, but I was determined to finish the job), that I noticed the small shelf to the side of the irons; which, I had supposed was simply to place hot pans on, but was in fact a 'swivel', hinged so that it would swing over the fire. With the irons done, I unhooked the cauldron, took it through to the slop stone, and used the remaining water to scrub it inside and out. Under the thin sheet on the mattress was a tartan rug, both the rug and the mattress were clean, so I would use my sleeping bag.

Unpacking my small camping pan from the car, I filled it with water and placed it on the swivel and went to bring in the remainder of the logs to dry. In the meantime, those stacked by the grate would suffice, supplemented with coal. Returning outside to shake the blanket from the bed, I placed it under the cushion on the low chair in front of the fire, upended the bucket, placed my tea and a packet of biscuits on it and sat down.

After watching the flames of the fire for a time, I took the case over to the table to begin the task of sorting through the papers. I soon discovered that most of the pads were numbered, and seemed to have some sort of index on the front covers. There were a few strays with no number or index, these I put to one side and piled the rest in numerical order. Of the loose sheets left in the case, there were no personal papers, envelopes, official documents or pictures, no identification whatsoever, even the letters had no addresses or signatures; not even a name. They were all written on white paper, many discoloured to varying degrees, but one alone looked like parchment; this was obviously the oldest, separated from the rest I would guess by several years, but written in the same hand.

In the process of removing my glasses to clean them, I glanced across to the front window and saw the moon rising. The fire was a weak glow, so I fed it some kindling followed by a small log it soon crackled and leapt back to life.

As dusk descended, with the exception of a handful of biscuits, I realised I had last eaten at the hotel, and felt a surge of unreasonable gratitude that I did not have to return there; for despite the hotel's efforts to make visitors feel at home, I would not miss the tiled bathroom, cheerful duvet, central heating, and all the other facilities it had to offer. A mattress on the floor and an open fire were far more welcoming. I unhooked the lamp and took it through to the slop stone to refill it, and felt a cold fine shower of rain on my back. It was blowing through the make shift 'window' above the shelf, and I quickly stuffed it with the plastic bags my shopping came.

While the soup heated on the swivel, I made some toast, recollecting far off days and my Gran's long handled toasting fork. The toast improvised as croutons as I sipped my soup slowly, relishing every mouthful, and could not have been more content, in fact would not have been as content, if I were feasting at an elegant restaurant.

Having finished my gourmet meal, with the remains of the biscuits and a mug of tea, I watched the fire until it was no more that a single red ember, drew the bolts across the doors, unnecessarily, and went to bed.

Chapter Seven

The next morning I awoke to absolute silence and a pale yellow sun, shining shyly through the window, as if looking on the inside of the bothy for the first time in a long time; and knew how Avylis was able to live here, content with the peace and simplicity. My feet landed on icy flagstones as I got up from the mattress and lit the fire. Waiting for the water to heat for a wash, I went outside to my 'fridge' for milk and other perishables stored in a box. Birds were busily looking for food and I broke up some bread as they swooped down for their unexpected manna.

Balancing bread against the irons of the grate, my egg and bacon cooked on the swivel, and with just one turn of the bread my breakfast was ready, deliciously seasoned with bird song and sunlight. Enjoying my second mug of tea, I switched my small battery radio on to hear two politicians being interviewed on the morning news, and immediately turned it off, resenting the intrusion. Picking my glasses and the sheet of sepia coloured paper from the table, I returned to sit by the fire and read:

His help and advice you didn't heed.
His understanding you didn't need.
You had no time for sympathy and care,
You scorned his courage, he hadn't been there.
He tried to help, because he knew the way,
But you were in a rush, wanted no delay.
So you left him behind in grief and despair,
Because he loved you then, and he really did care;

Yet what could he do on that dreadful day,
But watch your back as you turned away?
You knew all the hazards and pitfalls before,
And could cope with those, and even more.
The grief and the pain you would fight and win.
Oh! Never, never would you give in.

So you've reached the crossroads,
Don't know which way to go,
Don't look back for help, rejected so long ago.
Don't expect the advice, that's no longer there,
Remember... you left behind all the love and care.
No, don't place the blame on anyone else,
Now you feel bitter, alone and neglected,
After all, when you set out so long ago,
What had you really expected?

Did you really think you could do it all on your own?
Did you really believe you could travel alone?
Did you convince yourself your own tears you could dry?
Did you think you were able, over mountains to fly?
Now where's the confidence, when you'd said 'Yes, I know'?
Where's the self-assurance, of not so long ago?

So now choose the way that you want go,
Straight on ahead... it's downhill you know;
Or turn round and look back along the track,
But will the love be there when you get back?

He loved you then, and he loves you still;
But things will change as you walk back up the hill.
You'll have to learn to love and care, and try to understand.
You'll have to learn to offer an outstretched willing hand.
Do you still have the strength and the confidence still?
I think you have and I think you will.
Oh! Yes, you will still have your fights

and your battles to win,
But the hardest of all will be;
'Please can I come in?'

Who was this person who had ignored such advice, and set out so confidently? And who was the man offering it?

But their confidence was proved to be unfounded with the realization that they had 'run away' from love – lost it. Then the humiliation of having to admit that their misplaced confidence had dissolved - the decision to return - in the desperate hope they would be accepted back. That's not easy. Did they return? Were they accepted?

~ ~ ~

Remembering the paper I had found in the shirt pocket I read it again.

'My heart has at once been seared and calmed; wounds
open and raw have been soothed the instant you spoke...'

Both were written in the same hand, though it was difficult to imagine they were both original writings from the same source; and if they were what could be the connection? How does one proceed from the first to the second? Both spoke of struggle, heartbreak and love, and both ended with hope; but one thing was certain, Avylis was not the loner she appeared to be, no, there was or had been a significant man in her life, but who? And whoever 'it' was, there was clearly an intimate connection, for one at least was understood, almost to their core, by the other.

My thoughts were broken by the sound of heavy rain, and the awareness that I was cold. I backed the fire up with coal, pulled on another sweater and made a mug of tea. This was my first complete day in my newly acquired home and having decided to stay until the mystery of Avylis was unravelled, it was time to begin, and the beginning was the 'reporters' pad labelled No.1.

I had just finished reading the pad, and was reading my précis of it; when my eye was distracted, by presumably the same little mouse I had encountered yesterday. The mouse stopped, our eyes locked as we stared at one another. After explaining to the mouse, that as long as he had no intentions of inviting his friends to visit, he was welcome to stay, I moved to prepare lunch, leaving the mouse to ponder the new 'house rules'.

Chapter Eight

Apart from the villagers I had met two days ago, I had not seen anyone, but was under no illusion that they knew where I was staying, and that speculation would be gathering apace. It was necessary to take several factors into consideration; the loyalty the villagers held for Avylis, although this may be lessening after three years, until the subject was broached, as it had been by my enquiry at the village shop; the tenacity of villagers to get things sorted out to their own benefit, after all the people who had tried to buy the property had met with the impossible, according to the owner of the 'Buck Inn'; and, not least, the acceptance of in-comers. It is one thing to know I was here legally, quite another to be accepted, and that factor may be vital. Also I was quite aware that living here with no utilities, the place could soon be deemed uninhabitable, obviously not so for Avylis, but certainly it could be for me.

Wandering over to the window I slowly scanned the scene, the silence only broken by the gurgling stream and gentle breeze. There were no buildings, roads, or man-made structures on the skyline. It was difficult to believe that anybody lived within fifty miles let alone five. The effect of this was to believe my fears were unfounded, and, it being Sunday tomorrow, I needed to go into the village.

After calling at the shop for a paper, I went to the 'Buck Inn' and found myself, at least momentarily, more interesting to the locals than their ale, as we exchanged greetings. Normally I would have been naturally talkative, but for once my lips were sealed, prepared to be led rather than lead. The landlord's question required no answer.

"Hello again, still here then?"

Smiling, I ordered soup and went to sit down, as curious eyes watched my back. My presence may have gone unnoticed in summer but this was winter. Maybe it was my well-tuned imagination, but was the conversation at the bar now more restrained?

I was halfway through solving the crossword puzzle when a young couple arrived on a motorbike came in, and were acknowledged by all as they sat at the adjacent table to me.

The young man addressed me, as he pulled off his jacket. "Hi, awful day. Not the weather for walking."

I agreed, as he turned to his companion enquiring if she wanted the usual, but the young lady answered that she would have the steak and ale pie for a change and ended with, "Thanks Charlie."

My eyes went to the motorbike parked outside and back with interest to Charlie, a lean figure who stood over six feet tall in his leathers, and whom I guessed would be in his late teens, then to the ring on his companion's finger. Smiling I picked up my pen and returned to my puzzle.

On leaving, I enquired of Charlie and his companion where the church was. It was the lady who replied informing me that the church was in the next village and the service started at midday, adding directions, before informing me that they would see me there.

Chapter Nine

A cheerful lady greeted me, opening the door to the inner church as she handed me a hymn book and leaflet. The small building was welcoming with several bright banners hanging on the walls alongside children's artwork. A middle aged lady frowned with concentration and annoyance as she played the electric keyboard, as if trying to control a badly behaved child. The service proceeded with the intimations, which included a welcome to visitors and an offering of coffee after the service.

Following the conclusion of the service, the minister, who had a clear strong voice during the service, now spoke little above a whisper as he came over and asked if I had a drink. We were still talking when a middle-aged man approached and, after acknowledging me with a curt nod, proceeded to ask the minister, "What became of The Prodigal's brother?"

"We are not told. There is no further mention of him," the minister replied.

The man looked annoyed and stated, "Odd. Little point in a story with no end," and wandered off, leaving a look on the minister's face as if he had somehow failed abysmally.

"*It is common to be more eager about secret things, which belong to God, than about things revealed, which belong to us and our children; to be more desirous to have our own curiosity gratified, than to have our conscience directed,*" I said, "with apologies to Matthew Henry, if my memory is not correct." (Quote from The Interpreter's Bible, Matthew Henry's commentary from John 13 verses 36-38)

"Pity he was in such a hurry," the minister said, watching the man disappear through the door. "He may have left with something else to consider, however."

31

Chapter Ten

The next day, my only companion was Mick, my pet mouse, never being quite sure which of us was the lodger, and to whom I fed the odd chunk of cheese, (minus the accompanying trap), as I searched through the paperwork.

It appeared that at some point Avylis had decided to keep a detailed record and that was when she started to use the 'reporters pads', of which there were twenty-two.

These began by recording her journey to the Scottish Isles, and continued on through over a period of three years, giving an account of an itinerate, living in bothies, hostels, bunk houses, monasteries and for long periods in a tent. Never does she mention 'going home', as the record is so detailed that nearly every single day is accounted for. If she had a home it was uninhabited, at least by Avylis. Why did she lead a peripatetic life? Was it of necessity, was she escaping from circumstances, running away from actual or perceived danger, or was she simply trying to forget the past for some reason? Surely these possibilities would not account for her keeping such detailed records. I concluded, at least for now, that her lifestyle was of her own choosing, whatever that reason may have been; and if they were honest accounts, which I did not doubt, there was little I'd read so far to suggest that she was dissatisfied; on the contrary she seemed quite content.

The day to day diary, which for the larger part was the simple everyday occurrences, was written on one side of the pads only, some of the reverse sides had been used, but the two pieces I had read, seemingly had no connection to the diary, so I ignored them until I could place them within the whole.

Leaning back on the wooden chair, my shoulders and back complained, while my legs groaned at my attempt to move them. The wind was hurtling round my little shelter, finding entrances on all sides and there was only the faintest glow of embers in the grate. Pulling on another sweater, I resuscitated the fire and put some soup on to heat.

The window framed a picture of a desolate wild night, and I wondered where Mick was. Putting my anorak on, while summoning up all the fortitude I could muster to face the elements, I undertook the task with the firm resolve to keep the coal bucket well stocked in future.

Outside the wind blew the bucket viciously against my legs. Placing the torch between my teeth I filled the bucket and struggled back through the door, which instantly slammed behind me, and stoked up the little fire. As I went to top up the oil lamp, the carrier bags I had used to block the gap, flapped around like two white flags, no match for the enemy, and there was nothing else to block it with. Tomorrow I would look around the area for some suitable stones, purchase a small bag of cement and try my hand as a 'bricky'.

Chapter Eleven

The following morning dawned chilly, calm and bright, and on waking and propping myself up, I spied Mick sitting on the far corner of the table looking at me, and was instantly aware that he had 'got up' only seconds before; however, feeling somewhat guilty, as I was treating myself to breakfast at the café, and with no firm evidence of Mick's misdemeanour it seemed unjust to deprive him of his cheese.

Overnight, the frost had sketched an exquisite picture over the colours of the landscape. The strands of a cobweb stretched out stiff, slender white fingers; dormant trees were embellished with tiny white stars at the end of each twig, and brown leaves had been edged with frozen crystals. In the distance, against a pale blue sky, trees were held in the embrace of silver gossamer. It occurred to me that the demise of one season had not succumbed to hibernation, rather it had been metamorphosed, and lived. I crunched across the newly laid white carpet and picked up a stick to break the surface ice on the stream, for the birds. Switching the car engine on and pushing the back window defroster button, I squirted de-icer over the windscreen and left it to defrost. I broke up some frozen bread for the birds and moved my 'fridge box' indoors, there was now little difference between the two climates.

On the drive down to the café, I pulled over to let the 'post bus' pass. The post lady stopped alongside me and I enquired if she had to collect, sort *and* deliver the post for the area. She informed me that there used to be another postman who left, but she didn't' mind, and could get the job done quicker without others interfering, especially men. The post lady agreed the weather was cold, but cheerfully told me it was forecast to get much worse. A van pulled up behind and she began to edge forward, explaining that we mustn't make Andy late for work, barely disguising the intimation that some folk actually did work.

I parked outside the small café, arriving at the same time as the minister, who greeted me, remembering my attendance at church. As we walked into the café, the warmth encompassed and welcomed me, as if aware that I lived in the bubble of mercury, which remained stubbornly stuck at the base of the thermometer. The minister indicated the table with a reserved sign on it, as he removed his scarf and gloves, placing these in his coat pocket, which he then hung on the hook provided. Fearful of losing a single degree of this new found comfort I removed not a thread. As we sat down he asked what I would like to eat.

While pondering this offer, Eileen came over, automatically placing cutlery and a napkin in front of us both, as she said, "Morning Kevin, cold one today," and without waiting for a response, turned to me. "You here again, we shall be after putting you on our regulars list soon. Is that not right Kevin?" She smiled and winked at Kevin before asking me, "now, what can I get for you today?"

"Breakfast please?"

"Will that be egg, bacon and toast, or do you want everything?"

The 'everything' breakfast struggled to confine itself to the perimeters of the plate, consisting of two eggs, two pieces of Lorne sausage, two rashers of bacon, tomatoes, beans, mushrooms, black pudding, fried bread, toast, jam and tea; all served by the slim figure of Eileen. Mrs. Bea had been right, stick thin she may be but nevertheless a picture of health and energy. That's her natural physique, I decided, then glancing across the table at the perfectly proportioned, athletic figure attacking the food before him, I picked up my cutlery, and wondered when the much maligned fried breakfast would rightly be granted the accolade it so obviously deserved.

Left with only toast and tea, I remarked that the minister must feel encouraged to have a large congregation in such a remote area, and suggested he must be doing something right. He looked at me and then across the café into the far corner. I followed his gaze, uncertain if he had heard me or was simply thinking before he answered. All I could see above the heads of the other diners was a framed picture on the wall, but could not decipher what it was. Finally the minister turned to back to me.

"It wasn't always so, and I'm afraid you are wrong, it has little to do with me." He paused, looking directly at me, as if deciding whether or not to continue.

"Some time ago," he said, "a lady came to stay in the village. The villagers came to church to see her, not myself." There was no hint of self pity or bitterness in his voice, rather a look of sadness on his face. "The lady walked the seven miles to church every week, in all weathers, always declining the many lifts that were offered, sat at the back of the church, head bowed throughout the service. She left directly after the service, never staying for coffee but set off to walk back. Because she couldn't ..." his gaze went back across the room, "or had chosen not to speak, we never really knew anything about her, least of all what happened to her." The minister looked towards the window. "All I do know is that she always gave me the impression that she was completely at peace... had no fear... and a great understanding of others." He hadn't been unaware of me as he spoke, but searching for words, our eyes met as he said, "Sorry, I'm not making much sense am I?" Observing his struggle with the telling of his tale I remained silent, pondering the fact that it was three years since the lady had left, yet the congregation had not declined. The silence was broken by Eileen.

"Now can I get you two some more tea?" We both nodded, and after a quick glance at us she went off to replenish the teapot, leaving us with our thoughts. On her return, finding us still silent, she placed the teapot on the table and quipped, "Well, look at the two of you. You look as if you've lost a pound and found a penny." The response was a weak smile from the minister.

"I was just trying to explain about the lady," he said. Eileen scratched her cheek with one finger and drew in breath through pursed lips, looked at Kevin, and then as she faced me I took the opportunity to ask one of the many questions requiring an answer.

"How old was she, the lady?"

Eileen pursed her lips again and frowned before answering. "We often wondered, it was difficult to say, but judge for yourself," she indicated the picture on the wall.

The picture was of a wild looking person with long unruly brown hair, heavily flecked with grey, wearing jeans, black polar neck sweater and a green and maroon anorak; all of which looked two sizes too large. On her feet were brown walking boots. I took my glasses from my pocket and stood close up to the picture. The hazel eyes drew me into a deep peace, demanding my attention. I was totally captivated, unable to look away, yet also unable to mentally form the questions that demanded answers, because 'the lady' seemed to be questioning me.

"Who are you?" I breathed. Turning from the picture, aware that the watcher was being watched, I went across to the washroom, and holding the soap in my hands stared into my own eyes, before returning to the remains of my breakfast.

"Well?" The minister said.

"Well?"

"How old do you think she was?"

"Oh," I replied. "I really don't know; but I don't think it matters. Do you?"

I picked up my tea not expecting a response, but the minister explained that one summer a tourist had left a pack of photographs, which Eileen had kept under the counter, expecting that they would be claimed. They never were. Sometime after the lady had left, when Eileen was painting the café, she found the photographs and casually glanced through them before throwing them away. She found one of a group of people, but the lady must have inadvertently walked into the photo to one side. The villages had donated money to pay a photographer, who had taken a frame of the lady from the picture and enlarged her.

~ ~ ~

On my return to the bothy just before one o'clock, Mick totally ignored me, content to nibble his cheese. I replenished the fire and fingered the washing on the rack, which would be dry by morning, if it didn't freeze again; and with a mug of coffee sat at the table more resolved than ever to find the answers to my questions.

~ ~ ~

Stiff, chilly and tired, I glanced at my watch. With the exception of moving once to light the oil lamp, stoke the fire and make a mug of tea, I'd worked until way past eight o'clock. Standing, stretching and shrugging my shoulders, and too tired to cook, I made a sandwich and sat in front of the fire to consolidate what I had so far learned of Avylis.

From her diaries, Avylis was an itinerate traveller, rarely staying in one place for more than a few weeks, often only days. She regularly went to local inns where she would have a coffee, sometimes soup, and write. She recorded meetings, either pre-arranged or spontaneous, the latter often while she was at various inns, but there is no mention of the details of these. Had the minister been right when he had said of Avylis, that she may, 'have chosen not to speak,' but why?

Chapter Twelve

I woke early, released one arm from my sleeping bag and quickly replaced it, needing time to formulate a plan of action. My feet landed on the frozen flags as I dressed as quickly as I could with useless fingers. After several attempts I managed to light the camping stove, with hands fast turning into what threatened to be a uniform shade of purple. Attempting to take the top off my partly frozen water bottle, an operation eventually accomplished with my teeth, I splashed some water into the small pan to boil. Before doing anything else, it was necessary to get a semblance of warmth into my fingers, and I held them near the meagre flame, which was about as effective as trying to defrost the North Pole with a match. I dragged the sleeping bag from the bed and pulled it over my shoulders. Foregoing the first hot drink, allowing the steam to warm my hands, I refilled the pan and moved quickly to light the fire and put another layer of clothing on.

Mick raced across the floor, from where, and to where I knew not, and did not care; at least *his* blood was still circulating. The fire quickly sparked into life, encouraged by a double ration of kindling, as I sat with hands wrapped round a scalding mug of hot water.

Convincing myself that no one would notice the unwashed, I combed my hair and made my way to the encompassing warmth of the café to thaw out, leaving the fire to penetrate the icy air. Half way through my egg and bacon, I was struck with guilt. How could I have left Mick without his cheese, and about to gulp down my tea, admonished myself, 'Get a hold of yourself, it's only a mouse!"

On my return, half expecting to face a tirade on my selfishness, Mick was nowhere to be seen, as I broke off an extra large piece of cheese.

Refreshed by food and warmth, I continued my task. Amongst the loose papers was a thin purple covered notebook; the pages were like tissue paper, and as both sides had been used, it was difficult to read.

Alone, desperate and frightened,
Like a rabbit in a snare,
As I struggle for survival in this bottomless pit of despair;
But the steps to guide and the straws to cling to,
Are no longer there,
And the footholds crumble beneath me,
As my fingers grab at empty air.

I'm tired of talking and I'm tired of thinking.
I'm tired of looking and I'm tired of asking;
Because whatever I think and whatever they say,
I'm left with nothing at the end of the day.

I'm tired of hoping, expecting and trying,
When I know my soul is slowly dying.
I'm tired of sympathy, reprimands and encouragement,
When on my own destruction I now seem hell bent.

My usefulness, if ever there was any is now fulfilled,
The crop has been harvested,
And the land lies freshly tilled.
I cannot relive one dream, or one single aspiration.
Dead, the ambition, the incentive, the motivation.

I'm too tired, weary and despondent to care anymore.
I've lived my life and I've emptied the store.
Now I'm left without the grain, without the seed to sow,
And without that nothing will flourish, nothing will grow.

But you cannot reap and harvest if you have no seed,
And you cannot care if you have no need.
You cannot drain affection off others
For your own selfish desires,
So life gets tougher and one eventually tires.

All I am asking, is for one little grain,
That I can plant and care for and nurture;
That is all I need to ease the pain,
A little seed to watch it grow,
And ripen in the future.

The account continued telling of a ruthless, almost brutal, honest search, to discover the meaning for her life, which came close to destroying her on more than one occasion. This period was undertaken completely alone, in her belief that it was the only way, to truly understand who she was; and it led to her writing:

> *We emerge out of darkness into the undergrowth of life; but until we recognise the scythe, which enables us to cut a path through worldly knowledge and reason towards the light of wisdom, we remain in the shadows; but we have to beat our own path to freedom, and there are many crossroads.*

And later:

> *I looked at the well trodden, downhill, dead-end and circular tracks in the abyss in which I had been wandering, and realised the only way to glimpse the light was to climb upwards. But I could not climb up the track laden down and so it was I set out into the unknown; but no longer was I running away - but towards - for now I had a friend, a companion with whom to travel.*

A companion? But who?

Having exhausted the supply of logs which had been left, and with only half a bucket of coal it was time to go for more supplies. As I reached the village shop it was raining heavily, so I quickly stacked the coal in the boot of my car, and was just opening the car door when I heard a child's cry. I looked up and saw two girls. The older girl was trying to help the younger one, who had blood flowing down her face, to her feet. I went across to see what had happened. Reassuring them both as I took them into the 'Buck Inn'. Leaving the youngsters in the care of the owner I went back to the car for my first aid box. With the child in the arms of the owner's wife, I cleaned the wound and applied a dressing to hold the small cut together, and the bleeding stopped. After both tear stained faces and mucky hands had been washed, the landlady suggested they may like some chocolate ice-cream, both the youngsters faces lit up, while the rest of us shivered. Just as the children were tucking into their ice cream, while I drank my tea, an anxious grandma came in. She gave each of the girls a cuddle, before coming over to thank me. The eldest girl, Kate, explained to Grandma that her sister, Hannah, had dropped 'Boo', and had fallen. Grandma, at Hannah's request, examined every inch of 'Boo' very carefully to ensure that a further plaster was not required, and suggested that maybe they should take 'Boo' home and give him a bath..

Remembering the fire back at the bothy,I went to thank the owner's wife for her help, and to pay for my tea, but the tea was 'on the house'.

~ ~ ~

The afternoon was spent sorting though the loose papers, which now lay in three piles, depending on the discolouration of the paper, in an attempt to bring some order to them. It occurred to me, that if I were to find Avylis, I would first have to find her friend.

I went to bed reflecting on the day with the uppermost question in my mind being, had Avylis left before winter to find, or to go where she knew of warmer accommodation, in which case she could be back; but why had she left the bothy for me? But while I may, in time, forget most of this experience, I would never forget the peace I'd seen in her eyes in that photo in the café.

Chapter Thirteen

The next morning I awoke to a glowing fire, having set my alarm for two o'clock in the morning,when. I had leapt out of bed, put the ready prepared shovel of coal on the fire and leapt back into bed.

As dawn broke, I collected a bag of kindling, fed the birds, reminding myself to get them some fat balls and nuts, and filled the coal bucket. Snow covered mountains stood in splendid silence against a clear blue sky; the rising sun illuminated the skeletal trees in hues of oranges and reds; while the pure clear stream sparkled as it bounced along effortlessly..

I brewed a mug of coffee, and broke off a piece of cheese for Mick, ate it, and broke off another piece for Mick. Funny, I'd named Mick, determining his gender, on a whim. What if 'he' was a 'she'? For a moment I could hear the stampede of an army of paws demanding cheese by the round, and pondered if I should buy shares in an appropriate company, but I wouldn't know how. However, so far Mick had kept to the 'house rules', (or at least had the good sense to hold his soirées while I was absent), and I certainly had other things to think about; first of which I needed some food, so set off down to the café. Having finished my egg on toast I went to look again at the picture of Avylis.

~ ~ ~

Back at the bothy as I flicked through the mass of loose sheets the word, 'eyes' was looking back at me.

You found yourself looking into eyes that would transform your life. You were looking into unfathomable, imperturbable peace. Those eyes all knowing, yet so kind and gentle, drew you into their very depths. You would walk unerringly and unafraid, and had never felt so safe or strong in your life. You do not recall why you were standing looking into those eyes, but without an accompanying word, at least not one you can remember, they spoke of a deep understanding of peace.

Did this person have reason to be so calm and peaceful? One would think not, as daily they saw sadness, death, suffering and cruelty, and looked out on a world of despair. Was it because they were untouched by what they saw? You could not believe it, as this person worked tirelessly, and had done so for many years to ease the suffering that surrounded them. Was there respite at the end of the day, when they could leave it behind for a comfortable existence? No, they lived in the very midst of it and lived modestly.

Such calmness and serenity did not materialise from that, which the eyes looked upon, rather it shone out from within, and it was from within they found their strength and unshakeable peace. Few people are able to look upon this world with such assurance. Yet you believe it is possible, but you need the courage to fly above the realms of reason, and the faith to trust. Then, and only then, will you be able to close your eyes and look through the darkness into the light. So my friend, what have you learned from your travels?

After being too young to understand; trying to do what was expected of you; then running away, you finally confronted yourself. You learned that you must first find yourself. It takes courage, honesty and a long search; but you grow stronger along the way, strength required to hold fast to your principles, hope to continue, and yes, after what you have experienced, you surely have developed a sense of humour.

*Above all you will be able to look with a quiet confidence on
the world that once so troubled you. You will have found that
intangible precious gift in your life, peace.*

~ ~ ~

Who was this 'person', why no name? Was it Avylis's friend? No,
it was doubtful, as she had always referred to him as her 'friend,'
'companion' or 'guide' before.

Mick appeared from nowhere and settled on the mattress, (was
nowhere sacred?).

"Mick, you must be the *only* mouse who can boast of a house,
bed, and a fire, (which *couldn't* boast of providing heat), and an
endless diet of cheese, all rent free, do you know that?" I was
wasting my breath. "I need your help," I told him, "why would
anyone refer to somebody they obviously knew, as a 'person'?
Wouldn't it be usual to refer to them by at least their gender?
After all, you have a name I don't call you 'mouse' do I?"

I started to read the paper through again, until...

*'... it was from within they found their strength and
unshakeable peace.'*

"Unshakeable peace, Mick, isn't that what I saw in the picture
of Avylis, in her eyes? But *whose* eyes was she looking into?"

No answer was forthcoming. I gazed at Mick, fast asleep on *my*
bed "There is a theory," I began, "that hunger keeps us alert, so
as you are obviously overfed, I have no option but to reduce your
rations as of now." My threat went unheeded on Mick, still in the
hands of Morpheus.

I again focused on my conundrum, picking up where I had left
off, reading the paper to the end.

*Above all you will be able to look with a quiet confidence on
the world that once so troubled you. You will have found that
intangible precious gift, peace.*

The two words that had dominated my thoughts since I had first seen the picture of Avylis were 'peace' and 'eyes' and the two had become inextricably linked

Chapter Fourteen

Run towards, not away
If in this place you cannot stay.
When you arrive, you will meet yourself,
There will only be me, no one else.

What are you hanging onto here,
Except your doubt, sorrow and fear?
What will you find if you depart,
The deepest longing of your heart?

From all the tangibles you'll flee,
Your only companion will be me.
Can you cut free from all you know,
With only me the way to show?

No one to visit, no one to phone,
Will you depend on me alone?
Will you listen, will you heed?
Will you follow where I lead?

So I left, quite secure in my guide,
To find the meaning, not to hide....
And he led me to a peaceful place
Where I feel blessed very safe.

On the way we've laughed, talked and walked,
Across the hills, and by the streams;
And he has revealed, a faint glimpse,
Of what I yearned for, in my dreams.

Now I've just begun
Vaguely to understand,
Of who I am, and why I'm here.
Why I feel safe and need not fear.

He's always there when I call on him,
Gladly, joyously saying, "Come on in."
He listens, then speaks quietly to me,
Explaining how I can be free.

Free from doubt, anxiety and pain,
Nothing too difficult for him to explain.
I read the book he gave to me,
And write to him, 'to you from me'.

Your treasure lies not in silver or gold.
Not in anything you can touch, or hold.
Your treasure I have, and I will keep...for now,
Because it's a precious gift you seek.

But, if you want, I'll teach you my friend,
All you need to know and understand;
How to be sensitive, gentle and true,
And then I'll give all your treasure to you.

This appeared to be a two-way conversation. I returned to the previous sheet, which also read like a conversation. Just where did this leave me, especially as I picked up the next piece, which was clearly a letter?

My dear friend,

You know I struggle to love you, and that I take you for granted, neglect you, and do not make the effort to reciprocate your love. Yet, you also know that deep within me, there is a yearning - a void - that only you can fill.

But, through all my despair, confusion and turmoil, you have always been there; never treating me as I deserved but always drawing me back to yourself with love. You have reassured me countless times, lifting me out of my despondency, offering hope and joy.

Yet, I know, deep within, there is more. You may well ask what more do I want? What more can you give me? Why, when I know you have kept me from harm, supported me, made me aware, of your love for me...why my friend, Oh! Why, do I feel there is more, what am I asking for?

I came out here with you to learn to love you as you deserve; to look at the world through new eyes and to learn of love from you. As I started out on my travels, you blessed me with a period of absolute peace, when, in glorious weather, we walked through the countryside, over the hills and by the rivers, with an energy and enthusiasm I did not believe would ever be mine, and felt, for the first time in my life, utter peace and joy.

Maybe, it is because I feel inadequate that you protect me, keep me safe and secure, but I feel I give nothing in return. Do I really appreciate the love you shower on me, or do I take it for granted? It is also probably true, that I may, through all my confusion, try too hard, walk too fast, and in so doing overwhelm myself, to the point that it is all too difficult. I am impatient, and try to understand everything at once, yet feel I will never understand the depth of your love in its entirety.

Chapter Fifteen

Standing with a saw in my hand, deliberating whether I was up to the task, I was startled to hear the voice, and turned to face a lady, and instantly recognised the two girls with her.

"Hi," I said, placing the saw on the ground.

"I am Kate's and Hannah's mother, I do hope we are not disturbing you," the lady said.

"Not at all, I'm delighted to see you all, and pleased you brought Boo along."

The lady, whose daughters had the same dark brown eyes and long light brown hair, (Kate's tied back in a pony tail, and Hannah's plaited), looked around as if she had entered a preconceived environment and, having had her illusions shattered, was trying to re-focus.

"It certainly has changed." The mother, still looking around, was voicing her thoughts, rather than speaking to me.

"How are you two today?" I asked the girls.

"Go on," coaxed their mother. Hannah looked at her older sister Kate, who in turn looked at her mother, who stooped to whisper in Kate's ear

"Thank you for looking after us," Kate said, looking at the ground in front of me.

"Thank you for coming, to see me. Aren't you at school today?" Kate looked up and grinned.

"It's Saturday."

"Oh, silly me, of course it is."

"Look", Hannah, said, holding Boo up for me to see, "Grandma put him in the bath with lots of bubbles." And Boo, albeit a paler shade of blue, was certainly cleaner.

"Well, he looks nice and warm," I said, indicating his little knitted coat, and striped scarf. "Do you think he would like a biscuit?"

Hannah nodded enthusiastically, as her mother replied, "Well, maybe just one."

"Would you like a drink?" I asked the girl's mother.

"Oh, that's kind of you, but I'm afraid we must be on our way."

Leaving the girls throwing stones into the stream, watched by their mother, I went inside to get the required biscuits. On my return Hannah had placed Boo on the ground near the stream.

"Now you stay there," she instructed Boo. "Don't move until I come back. You're not to go near the water. It's *very, very* dangerous." She gave Boo, a stern look.

I was thanked by the youngsters for the biscuits, as their mother reminded them that grandma had cooked their favourite dinner and they mustn't let it get cold.

"Can we come again, mummy?" asked Hannah.

"Please?" added her sister. Mother looked at me.

"Well, in that case I shall have to go shopping for some chocolate ice cream, and what would Boo like?"

"Oh, he simply *adores* chocolate buttons!" We all looked at Hannah, who obviously knew Boo inside out.

"Chocolate buttons it is then," I said,

We shouted our farewells, as they walked down the track waving, and I turned back to my saw and the task in hand.

~ ~ ~

The thick branch, partly broken, hung at a crazy angle. Once I had managed to get a purchase with the saw on the wet wood and after several attempts at swinging on the branch, in an effort to elicit surrender, the branch screeched and fell to the ground, at which point I was tempted to shout 'timber', and stood back exhausted.

My reward for a job well done was to make some chips, and

sit by the fire contemplating the appearance of my first visitors, and still elated at my success as a lumberjack, before once more returning to the piles of papers.

> I walked in the company of the splashing burn, the songs of birds, and the whisper of wind in the trees. Sunlight lit my way, throwing a mantle of gentle shadows over the glorious forest floor. Higher into the forest the sun was dappled, as a lamp at my feet, and the silence was blessed.
>
> Oh! How I yearn to walk in the company of my friend, and for him to open my senses, to his love and peace. How I long for my restless soul to be calmed. What have I ever done to deserve to be loved, protected, and provided for in every way, knowing that I can never repay.
>
> But teach me, my friend, to appreciate you, as you deserve; teach me to empty my life of all the rubbish I hang onto, so that it does not distract me on my travels with you; teach me to forget my own cares and aspirations, to free me to the awareness of yourself, and reassure me that you will keep me in your sight; for sometimes I cannot believe you love me so much. Yet, in my heart I know that I am, at least in your eyes, worth the heartache I cause you. Teach me to enter deeper into the love you offer me; to understand the peace you have, and to live with you in that peace.

This surely was a friend who loved deeply; but from all accounts hadn't Avylis been loved, because she awakened love in others? Hadn't Gilbert said, 'she brought a sort of peace?...'

Mrs. Bea had been saddened that she could not do anything more to help her. The minister's congregation had risen during her stay. The villagers had had a collection to have her photo reproduced; and all this for a seemingly penniless stranger, little more than a tramp, always smiling, yet who never spoke a word;

but as Mrs. Bea had said, the villagers loved her, 'not out of pity, no, not that', so what was the reason? Whatever the reason was, the lady had certainly left her mark on this village, for she had been no casual tourist.

But was she the author of these papers?

Chapter Sixteen

The deafening noise was directly above me. I sat up, and then realised it was the rusty roof being buffeted by the wind. Getting out of my sleeping bag and pulling on my jeans and sweater, I lit the oil lamp. Using considerable force I opened the back door a few inches, only to be blown backwards as the door slammed shut, leaving the lower hinge useless, the lamp swaying drunkenly, and me looking like a well made snowman. From the window all was whiteness.

There was nothing to do but sit tight. The fire was still alight, it was just past three in the morning, and the noise was relentless, which, in a way was reassuring, as at least part of the roof was still intact.

I awoke to hear voices outside and a persistent rapping at the window. Only able to move slowly, painfully and with great care, having nodded off in the low chair in front of the fire; "Are you alright?" the young man shouted.

I nodded.

"It will take a while to get you out. We'll be as quick as we can," he informed me, pulling a balaclava back over his face and disappearing from view round to the back door.

~ ~ ~

The sun threw shadows over the drifts of snow; tree branches were heavily laden; only the tyre marks of the recently arrived vehicle scarred the whiteness.

I filled the cauldron, not knowing how many were outside, put the smaller pot on the swivel and made a drink, listening to the scraping of spades and the chatter of my rescuers. After about half an hour there was a shout from the door, and a burly young lad entered, introduced himself as Pete, and informed me they had finished. I invited them in for a hot drink, but he declined telling me to grab my coat, Eileen was preparing breakfast for us all; which was just as well remembering I only had one tin mug and a plastic cup.

Outside with my car wrapped in snow, I was told to 'hop in' to their vehicle and we moved off, with the men telling me not to worry, they would be back later to repair the roof and dig out my car; the main thing was that I was OK. I thanked my practical 'knights', who had arrived in a Land Rover, dressed in waterproofs and balaclava's. (A white charger no doubt would have made the journey; but I doubt armour, shiny or otherwise would have furthered the cause for rescuing me.)

~ ~ ~

The little village was a picture of industry; people clearing snow, gritting pavements and digging out vehicles. Children, joined by a few adults, were busy building snowmen, using anything possible as sledges and snowballing each other on a calm, sunny, icy morning.

Somebody had been busy in the café, where all the tables had been pushed together, doubling the seating capacity and two Calor gas heaters were at full blast. Several ladies, including Mrs. Bea, weaved their way between youngsters, distributing breakfasts, plates of toast and pots of tea. The reason for this impromptu gathering was a power cut, and Eileen, realising this at six o'clock in the morning had wasted no time in ensuring food and warmth for all. As in any emergency people had volunteered help. The elderly were escorted to warmth and food. Generators and heaters were provided, while the village stores had supplied extra food. It was a morning not to be forgotten, for its laughter, good humour and, what appeared to me, military precision.

After we had eaten and given a vote of thanks and three cheers for Eileen, my rescuers said they would see me later,they were 'off to get the vet, and help Harry with his sheep'.

The men each put five pounds on the table before leaving, and I did likewise. Eileen thanked me for my offer to help clear up, but said I mustn't stay too long, as from what she had heard I may be needed back at the bothy when the men returned. Hearing this, the minister said he was off to see a parishioner but would be back within the hour, and would run me back. I thanked him, as he explained, "It shouldn't be any problem, not now the lads have been down the track in the Land Rover, my car should make it. See you later then". There was a brief cheer as the lights came on, and promptly went off again.

~ ~ ~

Having cleaned up the café and placed the tables back to their usual places, the minister, stamping the snow from his shoes, entered looking dejected. Eileen immediately went to get him a cup of tea, and as I walked across to the toilet she winked at me as she poured a generous amount of whisky, from under the counter, into the cup, before severely rationing the milk. "That should do the trick," she said.

The ladies who had helped, had now dispersed, leaving the café empty apart from the minister and myself. Eileen suggested we may as well stay in the warm for a while, as she doubted the men would be back yet, and excusing herself disappeared into the kitchen area.

"You look as if you have more than your fair share of problems today," I said to the minister.

"No, not really. I've just come from visiting one of my parishioners in the next village, where fortunately they did not have a power cut. I'm fine." The minister, who I guessed must be in his forties, shared his thoughts with his tea for a few minutes.

"Do you know," I said, "I always remember a service I once attended when the vicar said that many a time, 'fine' should be interpreted as, 'Feeling Inadequate, Needing Encouragement'."

He thought about this for a minute, and then laughed. "Smart vicar," he said relaxing. "The truth is I've hit a brick wall with tomorrow's debating group. The person who was to oppose the motion has pulled out, and it is too late to postpone it."

"What is the motion?"

"Revenge is sweet."

"You chose that?"

"Goodness no. They are chosen by the parishioners. The group started several years ago to debate topical issues from a biblical standpoint, but recently..." his voice faded.

"And you personally cannot oppose the motion, of course."

"I'd rather not. I'm only there to..."

"Stop the blows landing?" I finished for him.

"Well let's hope it doesn't come to that." He smiled, but I detected an element of truth in my jest.

"If you are so desperate, I would be willing to do it, but I suppose, not being a villager, that would be out of order."

"Indeed not. Occasionally in the summer, it has been known, mainly in the holiday period, but the debates have always been open to one and all."

"Well then?"

"No, I couldn't expect you to take it on at such short notice, it is set for tomorrow."

"It really would be no trouble as I know what Av— the lady's thoughts on the subject are, and I agree with her views."

He stared at me. "You do? I didn't think you knew her." The minister clearly was confused.

"I never knew her. It's a long story, but if you—"

"Well in that case I would be most grateful. The debate is in the village hall at seven. I feel it only right to warn you that it may not be exactly what you are used to; that is, it's not exactly the Oxford Union and we take liberties with the presentation," he said.

"Well that's a relief." I said flicking imaginary sweat from my fringe, as the minister continued his explanation.

"There is simply ten minutes allotted to each speaker, a

show of hands for a 'seconder', followed by questions from the floor, which I think is five minutes, or is it ten, before a short conclusion from each speaker and the vote. So I hope you will not be disappointed. And now I must get you back, as I have a meeting in fifteen minutes."

~ ~ ~

The roof now had a new piece of corrugated iron over one corner. The door, which had been taken off, strengthened, and fitted with two new hinges, was back in place, and with my car able to see daylight again, I drove back to the village.

Seeing lights on, I went into the 'Buck Inn'. Hannah, who must have seen my car, ran over to me with a desperate tale of woe. Boo had fallen off the sled and now had a bandage on his knee. With appropriate concern I reassured her that if she left the bandage on, and took good care of him, he would soon be better. She assured me she would look after him, but she had told Boo, 'He must never, ever go on a sled, *never ever* again.' I agreed this was very wise and examined Boo, who fortunately had avoided any further bubbles, otherwise he risked disappearing in the snow, never to be found again. Hannah skipped back to her mother, swinging Boo upside down by his injured leg.

The men, having adamantly refused any payment for their work, insisting they had only patched it up with odds and ends, had gratefully accepted the arrangement to have a drink on me that evening.

On my return to the bothy, Mick was sitting on my sleeping bag, looking up at me.

"You've got precisely ten seconds..."

It had been a long day.

Chapter Seventeen

Routinely each morning I would light the fire, sweep and mop the floor, wipe the table, feed the birds and give Mick his cheese. The former part of this routine was because of the everlasting uniform layer of coal dust. However the task was no sooner finished than it reappeared, as if the shelter had been stripped of its clothes and immediately re-dressed. I had been negligent for a few days, and noticing that there were mucky fingerprints on some of the papers, which were difficult enough to read, the place was duly cleaned.

~ ~ ~

I arrived at the Youth Hostel, thirty miles away, produced my membership card and was afforded a shower and the use of the hostel's laundry room. Standing under the steaming water was a luxury, and also reminded me of the bitter cold I was becoming accustomed to. After emptying the tumble drier and folding my clothes as neatly as possible, I thanked the person on reception, and aware that they could not take any money for this kindness, put a donation in the 'Mountain Rescue Box' before I left.

The forested area not far from the hostel proved too tempting and, parking the car and putting on my walking boots, I followed the track.

An hour later and about to make my way back I lost my footing. 'Oh, no and I've just had a precious shower,' I despaired. However, as luck would have it, having fallen at an angle and landed on a huge rock, my clothes remained clean but my backside was complaining, which in the circumstances was preferable to dirty, wet clothes.

Driving back through the village, Mrs. Bea waved me to stop and so I pulled over and parked up.

"How are you?' she asked me with a concerned look.

"I'm fine, and yourself?' I enquired.

"Is it not too cold up there for you? Did the lads manage to repair your roof?"

"They did indeed, and made an excellent job of it."

"Yes, they're good boys. I'm glad I've seen you as I wondered if you would like to come round later. I have a big pot of stew in the oven, a little of which will do you no harm whatsoever, my dear. Peter tells me you have no cooker, how on earth do you manage?"

"I have my camping stove, and there is the swivel," I informed her.

"Camping stove indeed, wouldn't keep a bird alive," was Mrs. Bea's opinion on that.

"But, I am used to it," I gently protested.

"That's as maybe, but you can't cook a good wholesome stew on it can you?"

"No." I accepted defeat.

"So we will see you tonight then after the debate?" she commanded.

The debate. I'd completely forgotten, was it tonight?

Chapter Eighteen

Mick listened attentively as I read Avylis's thoughts on revenge to him, passing no comment, but at least he didn't nod off, so encouraged I put the paper in my pocket and left Mick to his own devices.

The community hall car park, with space for a dozen vehicles, was full, so pondering why it should be when surely most of the villagers would have walked the few steps to the building, I pulled up on the verge. There was, amongst various other notices in the entrance to the hall, a prominent one with details of the debate. My opposition was George Logan, while I was simply, 'A Visitor'.

There was considerable noise from the people the other side of the door, so taking a deep breath I entered a brightly lit hall, holding about fifty people on neat rows of chairs in front of the stage. Instantly a small group surrounded me, one of whom introduced me to the president of the society, who thanked me for participating, and confirmed the rules the minister had explained earlier. As we chatted, I overheard a whisper from behind, 'Well, this should be interesting'. Looking ahead, as we continued to talk, I smiled at the heads turned in our direction.

After excusing myself, I walked over to the toilets and overheard a lady's voice saying, "Can't see a stranger sorting him out."

"No," came the reply, "he needs a firm hand, not..." Unable to walk any slower, I never found out who had decided what I was not.

The minister arrived, and I remarked that I did not expect such a high attendance. He had a quick look around. "Well, tonight is, let me say..." he looked around again acknowledging people with a wave or a nod, "there is an unusual amount of interest in the debate tonight. Are you alright?"

I nodded.

"Good. Don't worry, they won't bite!"

By this time I was none too sure of this.

"Oh, and good luck," he added, and I had a feeling he *really* did mean it.

As I was thanking him, a lady approached me, saying that it was time to start and led me to a chair on the stage. I watched the well-built, balding grey-haired man, immaculately dressed in a navy suit and tie, walk with ease, straight-backed up the few steps and stride across the stage to his seat at the opposite side of the table to myself, en route acknowledging me with an apologetic smile.

The president, in her welcoming speech, turned to me, and explained that although it was euphemistically called 'The Debating Group' people mainly came to listen, as opposed to actively taking part. Then facing the audience again and slowly examining the people in front of her she continued, remarking that she could not understand why this should be, as she knew that there was no shortage of opinions. She allowed the laughter to abate before introducing Mr. Logan. Mr. Logan went to stand in front of the lectern, facing silence.

During the next ten minutes, Mr. Logan proceeded with his argument, mainly based on his understanding that God kept law and order by taking revenge on the 'evil' of this world, 'always had and always would'. He cited Adam and Eve; The parting of the Red Sea; Gideon; David and Goliath and on through to Judas. He summed up by stating that if righteousness was to prevail, then revenge must be taken against evil, and when triumphant, then 'revenge is sweet'. If in the face of evil people fail to have the *courage* to take revenge, then evil will overwhelm us.

I cast a glance at the minister, but his face was unreadable. The weak ripple of applause was heightened by three vivacious people on the front row, and the remainder left them to it.

I took my place at the lectern, acknowledged the president and the audience introducing myself as 'The Visitor' and began.

The room was silent.

~ ~ ~

"It is my intention to persuade you that revenge is deceitful, cowardly and selfish. Any sweetness there may be is but a thin veneer covering the bitter kernel of toxins within, from which there is no escape for those enticed by the honey coating." I paused, glanced down at the paper in front of me, and allowed the stifled exclamations to die down.

> "I suggest that anyone who is seduced by revenge will regret it. They start out with certainty, quite unaware that they have invited revenge to come and live with them, and indeed feed off them; for revenge is a parasite urging you on for its own needs and giving nothing in return. On the contrary, it eats away at your finances, time, self-esteem, health and much more, for revenge has an obsessive, insatiable appetite.
> It will, given the opportunity, destroy you, and only then, on reflection, will you realise you have traded peace for despair; and your only friend, revenge has long ago left you for another, for the time being; because at the beginning you were stood on the top of the hill, with fresh air around you, health, friends and family; but much more than these, hope. Now you are left at the bottom of that same hill lying in a desolate heap, without the resources to climb back up. For revenge who had urged you on down the hill, has no use of you now.
> If, however, you should be satisfied with the result of your action; will you feel 'justified'? Revenge is totally selfish, only concerned with its own needs. When its needs are met, when it has sucked every drop of life giving sap from your body it will move on; but, if you begin to rise again, it will return to haunt you. Revenge will constantly remind you that it is entirely due to your action that the alleged perpetrator of the crime is serving punishment. However, as it is unlikely you

*will ever know the full extent of your revenge, you may always
have doubts, fears and regrets that you will have to live with.
If we are honest we have all succumbed to revenge, and as a
result later realised we have behaved recklessly and regretted
our actions.*

*In the short term, the perpetrator, as you perceive them to be,
is punished, and then released to their freedom; but in the
long term your ally and short-lived friend, revenge may punish
you more cruelly. For long after the perpetrator has served
their punishment, you may well remain under sentence, with
no perpetrator to accuse but yourself.*

*If one were to pursue this course of action then whatever may
be the outcome they would ultimately be the loser, for true
justice has no ears for blame or revenge.*

Love and be happy. Hate and be bitter. The choice is yours."

I folded up the paper as I concluded, and fielded one question
from the floor:

"Isn't justice only kept by those *courageous* enough to take
revenge?"

I addressed the questioner, sitting in the front row, wondering
if he would listen now, for he obviously hadn't so far.

"As a child I learned a valuable lesson from my father, two wrongs
do not make a right. Let us not confuse justice with revenge. Justice
is governed by the laws of society, based on morality for the benefit
of all. Revenge is a personal vendetta governed by individuals with
the sole intent to inflict harm on others. If revenge were to govern
society, then the weak would be rendered powerless, little more
than slaves, leaving only the strong, who would presumably then
proceed to take revenge on each other. Justice may not be perfect,
but do we want to live in a society that attempts to be fair and
peaceable, or to let revenge have free reign? What happens when
the avenger is avenged? Where does it all end?"

I thanked the audience for listening and turned to take my
seat, to silence. Then a shout of, 'Exactly'; followed by a ripple
of claps; another shout of, 'Well said', as the ripple grew into full

bodied applause. Once seated, I kept my eyes on the Emergency Exit sign above the far door. The proceedings were brought to a conclusion by the President, at eight o'clock; the rest of the evening being given over to refreshments.

I made my way through the hall, acknowledging handshakes and compliments, as quickly as politeness allowed; and sat in my car for several minutes, thoroughly aware by this time that inadvertently I had taken part in a private feud, of which I knew nothing; but my uttermost fear was had my quest to find Avylis, been damaged? Had I inadvertently become a player in the feud, and if so would the villagers be so forthcoming towards me.

Chapter Nineteen

I delivered myself into the comforting warmth of Mrs. Bea's cottage shortly after the debate. Mrs. Bea ensured I was comfortable, explaining as she did, that Kevin would not be long.

"Oh, I hope I'm not intruding?"

"Goodness, no, my dear, Kevin always comes for his dinner after the debate, and also sometimes on Sundays, following the service. Someone has to make sure he eats decently. Men neither know how nor care to cook. Can't leave him to starve now can we? Mind you, his wife was an excellent cook, but in all fairness to the man he couldn't have known she would be taken so young. All that running he does is all very well, but you can't keep fit on fresh air." It was perfectly clear to Mrs. Bea; either feed the man or watch him fade away into the ether.

"Now tell me," Mrs. Bea said from the kitchen, "how was the debate? Did you carry the night?"

I thought for a while, but Mrs. Bea wanted an answer.

"Did you win?"

We were interrupted by a knock at the door, as Mrs. Bea shouted, "It's open."

Kevin entered greeting us both and removing his coat. Mrs. Bea carried in a large ovenware dish and placed it on the table, instructing us to help ourselves while it was hot. When we all had served ourselves to a hearty meal of stew, dumplings, potatoes and vegetables and Mrs. Bea had placed another log on the already flaming fire, the minister said 'grace' and we began our meal.

Mrs. Bea opened the conversation asking, for the third time, if I had carried the evening's debate.

"She certainly did," replied the minister, "by quite a margin."

"Well now, there's a thing," said Mrs. Bea, looking at me, "congratulations."

I looked at the minister as he swallowed and said, "She did very well indeed, especially at such short notice." He had another mouthful of food and continued, "almost took the roof off the place."

The interchange between Mrs. Bea and the minister felt to me as if they were discussing somebody else, for when I had sat down after my part in the debate, my thoughts had been concentrated on more serious matters.

We congratulated our host on her cooking, and all sat round the fire. I looked carefully at the bone china cup and saucer Mrs. Bea was handing me with trepidation, took it, thanking her, and immediately placed it carefully back on the table at my side. The minister with a whisky, probably in an equally expensive glass, apparently had no such qualms, and showed no sign of parting with it until it was empty, hugging it to his chest.

"Well, my dear, from what Kevin tells me," said Mrs. Bea, "you are being very modest."

"Oh, not really, it's just that, at times, I felt that the debate should have been held at the High Court, or in your case, maybe The Sheriff's Court," I suggested, " rather than the village hall."

My two companions looked at me and then at one another, which gave me my answer, but I left the subject, as I had no wish to place them in a difficult situation. "In any case," I continued, "it had little to do with me, the lady carried the evening not me."

Mrs. Bea stared at me, a cloud of suspicion drawn across her normally friendly open features. There was silence, while all our amorphous thoughts became clearer and lined themselves up in an orderly fashion. It was Mrs. Bea who broke the silence, quietly, but with a hint of brusqueness in her words.

"Did you know the lady then?" Her face had changed, becoming unreadable. Maybe she was genuinely puzzled, or maybe she felt I had betrayed her; but, I knew I was treading very thin ice. She had been open with me on our first meeting, helping a stranger in every way she could; maybe she felt she had already divulged too much. As I watched her, she gazed at her mantelpiece.

Having already decided during the meal that I was in the company of the two people who could help me the most in my search for Avylis, and they were both trustworthy, I said, "I can only tell you what I know of the lady which is precious little."

I proceeded to tell them of events, from my meeting at the ferry with Mr. Hodgson, to finding the papers, but omitting Avylis's name. (Avylis, could have made it known to them, but she didn't, so neither would I). Both listened to my short tale without interruption, as I finished, "strange as it may seem, that is exactly what brought me, and has - so far - kept me here."

They both looked at me and after a tense pause, I exhaled, unaware that I had held my breath, when it became clear that they believed my implausible story. During the next hour or so, all our questions tumbled over each other, with many interruptions, until well after ten o'clock.

Having arranged to pick Mrs. Bea up the following afternoon, as she was curious to see where the lady had lived, and suggested afterwards we went out for lunch; partly to repay her hospitality but mainly as I had one vital question which, hopefully Mrs. Bea could answer; for if she couldn't...

~ ~ ~

Mick's cheese was barely nibbled, and as I glanced around for him, noticed my chocolate bar on the table.

"Let me remind you," I said to the empty room, "this café has a set menu; it is *not* 'a la carte'."

Sleep evaded me for a time, as I recalled the evening's conversation, but on reflection most of the information I now possessed was divulged by Mrs. Bea, with the minister interjecting to confirm or to question Mrs. Bea about the lady. Avylis had, according to Mrs. Bea, stayed in the village for two years, a long time for one accustomed to a nomadic lifestyle, and apart from her occasional visits to the shop and church extremely lonely.

Neither her friend, nor anybody else visited her; this, I was now sure of without enquiring, because the villagers would certainly have known. After all, I now knew that someone had checked the building to ensure I had not broken in shortly after my arrival. Avylis only left the village, or simply had not gone into the village, for a few weeks before her final visit to the shop; when Mrs. Bea had commented that she looked thinner yet stronger. Had she been ill? I could not help but feel that Avylis had indeed left the village during that period, but why, and once she had left, why come back, apparently only for one day? If Avylis, had been ill and had gone away, where had she gone? And anywhere was a long way on foot, especially if she was ill. If this was the case, she indeed was a courageous, determined lady. I was certain she would not have ventured into the village, and risk being seen, if she had been ill. Yet, how did she leave without being seen, for even at night there were eyes everywhere.

Chapter Twenty

Mrs. Bea was ready when I called the following day, putting on a thick woollen coat, scarf, gloves and hat, before facing the icy wind. It was only a ten-minute drive and I had ensured that the fire was blazing to its full height and left hot water simmering on the swivel; though what Mrs. Bea would think of a teabag in a mug, I shuddered to think.

I drove up the track slowly, as my silent passenger seemed to be absorbing every detail. When I stopped outside the bothy, Mrs. Bea stared around in disbelief and said, "Good gracious, I would hardly have recognised the place."

"You're the second person to say that," I said, explaining about the girl's mother, as I opened the car door for Mrs. Bea, but allowed her to get out of the car unaided. "Despite the weather she stood perfectly still looking at the scenery, and then the outside of the building, clearly finding it difficult to come to terms with what she viewed. Eventually she turned to me and I walked over and opened the door to the bothy, for her.

"I would give you a guided tour," I joked, "but as you can see it all from one spot... but please take your choice of chair," I said apologetically, "and I'll make you a cuppa."

Mrs. Bea had not said a word since entering, but chose the higher of the two chairs to my relief, as I only had one blanket, which had become accustomed to its new identity as a cushion.

"Thank you," Mrs. Bea said, with a sad smile, as I handed her a mug of tea, but it was obvious that she was still struggling with her own thoughts.

"This place was never meant to live in," Mrs. Bea uttered,

speaking her thoughts aloud, as she looked around. We sat in silence for a while sipping our tea, until Mrs. Bea turned her head, stayed perfectly still, and stared towards the gap in the wall. Following her gaze I closed my eyes and prayed, before clapping my hands and Mick disappeared. Mrs. Bea put her mug down, and I took my opportunity.

"That chair is not very comfortable," I smiled, "believe me *I know*; but alas, this one is even worse! Should we abandon both and go for lunch?"

~ ~ ~

We were greeted at the Malt Bottle Inn by a smiling, young gentleman, with immaculate styled black hair, clad in a maroon waistcoat over a snow-white shirt, black trousers, and polished shoes. He helped Mrs. Bea with her coat, and taking my jacket, led us to a window table.

The inn welcomed its visitors with a roaring log fire which gave the oak beams a warm glow, and threw a youthful radiance on the faces on all those gathered.

Tables, covered with red linen, were adorned with, shining cutlery, white linen napkins and sparkling glasses. Central to all was a small glass vase of freesia, adding a discreet flash of colour. Bottles stood on highly polished shelves at the well-lit bar, while glasses hanging overhead twinkled like miniature galaxies in the firelight. The scene was bold indeed, compared to the soft lighting by the tables.

We dined on the roast beef and Yorkshire pudding as we discussed the food, the inn, and the music playing quietly in the background; which Mrs. Bea informed me was Mozart, almost certainly played by the Amadeus Quartet.

Afterwards we settled back into the well-padded armchairs for our coffee.

"Have you been here before?" asked Mrs. Bea.

I shook my head and explained that I had spotted it a few days ago and had taken a chance, but she clearly appreciated it, saying that it wasn't often she ate out these days.

"So, what did you think of the cottage?" I asked.

"Cottage?" she queried, "your so called cottage, my dear, was never meant to be lived in. It is a bothy, where the shepherd used to stay, and to store fodder for the sheep." She smiled and I allowed her to continue, hoping I would learn something new. "You see in winter, the shepherd would have lived up there to keep an eye out, during heavy snows and stormy weather, when the sheep sometimes got into trouble; but mainly at lambing time. You have to remember, we haven't always had tractors and the like."

I watched Mrs. Bea, her silver hair coloured pink in the firelight, dazzling Lazulite eyes, and deep laughter lines, listening to the lilt in her laugh. It was impossible to judge how old she was, but I knew from the news cutting on the wall of the post office that she was now in her mid- eighties; for the news cutting was from the year she was awarded the OBE, for services to the community.

The waiter came across, and we ordered more coffee.

"Have you no idea whatsoever who gave it to you?" Mrs. Bea asked.

"None at all. What I can't figure out is why she left without somehow informing someone in the village. From what I understand the villagers liked her and she them, and it just doesn't seem to fit that she wouldn't have found some way to let them know she was leaving."

"Is it important?" Mrs. Bea asked.

"Maybe. To be honest it's rather critical to my trying to find her, or at least understand who she was. I believe she had a friend who she was very close to, but he would be, even if it were possible, more difficult to track down, as I don't believe he ever visited the village," I said.

"Oh, no. We would have known simply because, as you know, there is only the one road into the village." Mrs. Bea frowned then added, "I suppose there is a possibility that she may have had a visitor in the summer when there are more people about... but no, no it's unlikely," she concluded dismissing the possibility. We sat in silence, before she ventured, "You say if she had found a way to let us know she was leaving it may help?"

"Yes it would."

"Well, it's not much, and I'm not sure it will help but I may have something."

Finding it hard to believe, that she may *just* have the one thing I needed, and unable to dampen my new-found hope I enthused. "*Anything*, anything at all would help, believe me."

Mrs. Bea smiled at my obvious delight, but tried to temper my enthusiasm a little. "Well I really do not think it will be much help but if we go back, I could show you." For a minute my spirits dropped, was she going to show me the small picture of the lady I had noticed on her mantelpiece, probably unaware I'd seen the one in the café?

"Come on then," she ordered, with an enthusiasm to match my own. After thanking the staff of the inn we drove back to Mrs. Bea's.

Mrs. Bea instructed me to make myself at home, and with agility belying her age, disappeared upstairs without even taking her coat off. Returning to her living room she handed me a scrap of paper. I read: 'Thank you, Good Bye.' I almost went to hug Mrs. Bea, who asked, "Does it help?"

"Indeed it does," I said, with a huge grin. "Thank you so much."

"Well now there's a thing," she said. I looked at it once again, and handed it back to her, thanking her again for showing it to me.

"When did she give it you?"

"She didn't, I found it under the milk bottle holder the day she left."

"Who delivers your milk?"

"Oh, I phoned Len, my dear, as soon as I found it, but he told me that, that week he had to make his deliveries earlier as his farm hand was injured. He said he hadn't seen anybody, not even Ken, out on his morning run." Mrs. Bea looked at me expectantly. "Will it help you find her?" Now it was my turn to temper Mrs. Bea's optimism.

"It will be a lot easier with it than without it."

"You can take it with you, but please let me have it back."

"I promise to return it tomorrow, and thank you."

After Mrs. Bea had thanked me for showing her the 'er... cottage', and for the lunch, and I her for showing me the paper left by Avylis, I returned to the... just what was I to call the little place now? Playing around with the idea I decided on 'Bothcot.' It was an 'up-market' bothy; but certainly wouldn't impress the powers that be who dish out 'Stars' that meet desired conditions for residences.

Chapter Twenty-One

There had always been the unanswerable question, had Avylis written the papers now in my possession? I carefully unfolded the fragment of paper with those three precious words on and placed it on the table alongside the other sheets. At first glance it seemed to match, but trying to contain my excitement I sat down and compared it closely, picking out the formation of different letters.

I now had the answer, Avylis had written them, but the answer only led to other questions; why had she never sent the letters to her friend; why were the letters from her friend in her own hand, and why did some of the pieces written, appear as if each were writing, one questioning, the other answering? Had this new-found piece of evidence helped me at all? Feeling dejected I watched Mick, asleep under the window, no further on than the first day I arrived. Not knowing how to proceed, yet my determination to do so, outweighed my present mood to let go, where did I turn next?

I had exhausted, it would seem, anything the villagers could tell me about Avylis, but in pursuing this course of action had been, too often distracted from trying to untangle the many papers she had left. How long had I been here, two...three weeks? Action was needed as I could not stay in the bothy much longer, and *all* I had to help me now were the papers.

My Dearest Friend,

I have ignored you, yet you spoke to me, and yes I heard but paid no heed; wondering why you should listen to me anymore, and ashamed to come. I then determined to answer your call and ask for forgiveness. Yet, tonight, all my good intentions lie in the dust; I had found other things to do with the day, while I could still hear you calling.

You love me so much, yet I refuse to spend a few minutes a day to sit and talk and listen to you; you, who can strengthen me, give me peace and joy. I am utterly selfish. Yet, as I sit and think about these things, it occurred to me that I could not win this battle. I could not find peace, because as hard as I tried I could not tell myself that it did not matter and forget you for a while; no I couldn't justify my actions or thoughts. I simply couldn't come to terms with the fact that I had ignored you, in the certain knowledge that you love me so much, and that without you I would be completely alone and lost, but most of all afraid.

I came to understand that while I was fighting so hard to go my own way, I was losing out to love, your love; love that now returned, with arms to embrace me willingly with understanding and love, asking nothing. It was as if I refused to fight so you fought for me. Why? Because you didn't want me to travel my own destructive way, you did not want to lose me?

This made me feel woefully inadequate, selfish and lazy, but most of all ungrateful; but it also gave me the reassurance that you were there, would listen and accept me back.

Why I leave you, why I ignore you at times and why I choose to go my own way is a mystery to me; when paradoxically I know you are the only one who protects, teaches and guides me. It is as incomprehensible as an infant pretending it can manage without its mother.

When I do thank you for your goodness to me, however frail my gratitude may be, you give me peace, joy and love in *abundance. You do not withhold them, ever. But when I decide to try and travel alone, I am simply saying that I don't want these gifts, and in refusing rob myself of them, how foolish; and who else but you would keep these treasures safely, and then return them so willingly.*

Without your love I wander in misery, wondering why life is so bleak and forlorn. So I spoke to you, listened to you, asked for forgiveness, and then slept peacefully.

Why should anyone who knows they are loved choose to ignore it – walk away from it – knowing that there was no escape, especially when they had no desire to escape. Why not accept the love and be happy, instead of ignoring it and ending up miserable?

I stretched my legs out under the table, leaned back in the chair and clasped my hand behind my head, as I addressed Mick. "I'm supposed to be finding answers Mick. Well I hardly need to buy a folder to keep those in do I? You could file them away behind your whiskers. On the other hand I'd need an office, filing cabinets and staff for the *questions* piling up."

'Escape,' I mused, did they feel trapped... smothered?

"Oh, I don't know," I admitted to Mick, as I stood up, "I'm off down the café for a bite to eat, and I'll get you some choc. Do you want dark or milk?"

No answer.

Chapter Twenty-Two

My Friend

Without forgiveness each wrong you do steals a little bit of your soul in which to find a home; a little piece of your mind to distract you; and slowly steals away your self-esteem, so after a while you are taken over, your life is no longer your own. Your life has been infiltrated by guilt, fear and doubt; each move in, and each is heavy, but you have to carry them, and the burden grows heavier each day. While you live in this state, you constantly attempt to regain your peace, because without forgiveness, that is exactly what you have lost. You become nervous, worried, fearful, distracted and hurried.

Forgiveness heals by lifting your spirits, removing the shame, guilt and anxiety; that is, all those things that have been living with you, gnawing away at your mind, heart and soul, are evicted, bringing peace.

Do not punish yourself once you have been liberated, for you will find that I will treat you far more leniently and much more constructively; for your justice leads to self hate and despair, and you continue to feel guilty.

Trust me, you are safe. You may be unaware of it; you may not understand it; you may not believe it; you may even refuse it... and yet I love you, and there is nothing you can do to alter that.

True love can do no harm, as it hasn't got the capacity. So how do you follow the way of such love? Love is within you, imprisoned, until you choose to acknowledge it, and release it.

Two people corresponding. It was possible that one may have kept copies of their own letters, but surely they would have kept the original letters sent to them? There would be little point in copying those, and in any case why destroy the originals? Or had Avylis kept records of conversations with her friend? Yet how could she if her friend never visited, at least not while she stayed here? The only thing that was certain was they were all in her handwriting, and judging from the various degrees of discolouration of the papers, over a period of time.

But had she written any of them at the bothy, and if not, then why did she require pads and pens? Even if she had written letters while she had stayed here, it is almost certain that she never posted any, neither would she have received any; for these would have had to be directed via the post office, and Mrs. Bea would surely have mentioned that fact.

Just how did this friendship survive for two years with apparently no contact whatsoever? Or had she isolated herself deliberately, and if so it would not appear to have been the result of desperation. Had Avylis left the bothy to go to her friend? Was her friend still alive? Was her friend aware of where she had stayed?

I reached, absentmindedly, for a chocolate, had I eaten them all? Then I heard the faint sound of rustling. Mick was sitting under the table, oblivious of watching eyes, nibbling peacefully, as I wondered if it was worth writing to the manufacturers regarding the flimsy wrappings they used on their products.

With no coal left and only two small logs, I took the saw and axe outside, returning for my anorak, as it was drizzling. The rain rapidly grew heavier so I returned inside with a few sawn pieces and trusted that the stone floor would withstand a few heavy clouts from the axe. After placing the logs by the fire to dry I brought the remainder of the wood undercover remembering my first elation as a trainee lumberjack; now it was simply a task which had to be accomplished. I felt weary as I sat and listened to the rain clattering on the roof, but self-pity hadn't the wisdom to answer questions.

I looked forward in anticipation of attaining my desires, in the belief that they would bring me peace; but the anticipated peace has always proved elusive. Eventually I am weighed down with despondency, unable to chase after the next desire. I had refused to acknowledge that my desires were misguided; or that each failure had become a burden. Ultimately I had failed to recognise that while I chased after peace, I could not live in peace. So where is this enduring peace, which will not surrender to hopelessness, to be found?

I had to be prepared to stop, unload the burden, throw away my failures, disappointments, and my own desires; and then I could be at peace, because, I had realised, that all I needed was faith to trust in love, freely given, and in that trust depend.

"My only desire is to learn a little more about Avylis. That's all I want. Is that asking too much Mick? Should I be looking for her... or is my decision to do so going to leave *me* with a burden?"

Mick sat perfectly still.

"Do you know," I informed Mick, "I wish..."

'Wish... that's a desire isn't it?' I thought. Mick hadn't moved, but his tiny eyes still looked at me. "Anyway," I restarted, "I just...wonder if you wouldn't be more help to me if you had an expression on that little face, as it's impossible to know whether you agree or disagree; condone or condemn." I sighed as Mick, scuttled away. Mick was wise; I knew he understood every word I said and was fully aware that our IQ's were at opposite ends of the scale, and that I was just too dim to ever differentiate one of his 'squeaks' from the next. Moreover he also knew I had to find the answers for myself. One day I'd have to introduce him to Mr. Hodgson, they'd get along just fine.

Chapter Twenty-Three

What was that? Surely not the roof about to leave its moorings again?

No, it was someone knocking at the door. I opened it and looked at the young man, dripping wet, saying something, but I interrupted and ushered him in. Taking his wet jacket, I threw it over the rack, seated him by the fire and put water on to boil.

"Now what on earth has bought you out in this weather?" I enquired.

"I do hope I am not intruding, name's Damian," he said.

"Not at all Damian, pleased to see you," I reassured him as I made mugs of tea, "here, this will warm you up, and your jacket will dry a little by the fire. How did you get here?"

"Oh I was fortunate, Joe, saw me and threw my bike on his truck, so I didn't have to cycle far."

"Well, now you are here, what can I do for you?

"I did hesitate about coming. Maybe I shouldn't have." He looked down at his hands.

"Well I'm glad you did, I don't get many visitors and it can get lonely. After all, Mick's not much of a conversationalist'."

"Mick?"

"He's my lodger, eats cheese and chocolate." I indicated Mick's favourite corner.

"A field mouse." He laughed out loud.

That's better. I thought, joining in his laughter.

"I used to keep one under my bed as a child, that is until my mum found out and he was removed to the outhouse," Damian relaxed and continued, "I was at the debate on Wednesday, you were very good."

"Not me," I replied, "I was speaking someone else's thoughts, not that I didn't agree with them, but I didn't write it, merely read it," I said and answered his puzzled look. "Did you know the lady?"

He nodded.

"Her thoughts not mine," I continued.

Damian looked up, making eye contact for the first time, but did not refer to my question when he spoke.

"I came to ask if you would like to join us at a series of meetings we are holding at the church each week, when people can, if they wish, present one of their own reflections, which we can discuss. Not everyone will bring one, nor is there any need, some will just come to listen - I usually lead such meetings so it will be a pleasant change for everyone not having to listen to me - and after hearing your thoughts on revenge at the debate I came along to ask you..." (I took a breath for him as he ploughed on), "oh, sorry I should have told you, I'm the curate at St. John's which I am afraid is twenty miles away – right on the edge of the diocese - but I could always arrange transport if you wish and we do have a hot-pot dinner after." He finally stopped and his eyes, which had flicked about constantly, focused on me. The young man had spoken with an uncompromising enthusiasm, but seemed to lack the confidence to back it up.

He looked young, yet he must have been in his late twenties, probably a bit older, with high cheek bones, straight nose, jet black hair, grey-blue eyes, and regular white teeth The dimple in his right cheek only served to accentuate his handsome features.

"I'm really tempted but I am afraid that I really must sort out that lot," I explained indicating the papers. "It's my only way of finding out about the lady."

"It looks like quite a task," he said looking across at the pile of papers.

"Tell me about it, I sometimes feel someone has left me the whole of the Bodleian Library to read through." I watched as hope vacated his eyes, and felt an overwhelming desire to help him.

"Are there any guidelines for the reflections?" I asked.

The young curate thought for a moment. "No," he drew the word out slowly, and watched me, before he continuing, "as I said, after hearing what you said at the debate, I would have liked to have you on-board." Then he hurried on, "To be honest, my Vicar was taken ill suddenly and is expected to be off sick for three to four weeks, and I don't want to let him down while he's away." He stopped, and continued to fiddle with his nail bitten fingers, unconsciously.

"Well, as I have explained, what I said at the debate, I found in the papers. So, as I have a library at my disposal and if there is no specific theme for the reflections..." I said, walking to the table and shuffling through the papers, "I believe - yes, here it is. I'm willing to make a copy of this at the shop if you could use it."

I handed over the sheet of paper, and refilled the mugs as he read.

The palette of dusky oranges, pinks and mauves, splashed across the horizon, drifted slowly, relinquishing its transient splendour to the brightening morn, as the unseen artist sketched a mountain onto the skyline.

Below, the fishermen guided at night by stars, now watched as the burnished red carpet, unfurled at dawn across the lake, wrapped itself around the waves in their wake, a few threads escaping to dance atop the ripples.

As the fishermen secured their harvest safely in the harbour, the daily bustle of the shoreline was underway. Caravans of camels, men with laden donkeys, women, burdens balanced on heads with babies bound to backs, all vying for position in the overcrowded market place to trade their wares.

Fishermen landed their catches, and tended boats. Nets were repaired quickly and deftly with strong fingers of those accustomed to the task. Along the shoreline groups squatted round fires built on rough stone hearths, cooking and smoking; and all the time boats pulled ashore, each demanding space on the busy scene.

Nostrils were assailed with salt, dung, fresh and rotten fruit and vegetables, spices, fish, and smoke. Ears were awakened to traders haggling to sell their wares. Livestock grumbled, or murmured content with food and rest. Children laughed, squabbled and cried, and everywhere the shouts of people to make themselves heard above the tumult.

Slowly and quietly onto this scene came a man, unnoticed, but he noticing all, as he walked amongst the throng of humanity. He watched the wealthy traders, whose only cares were to amass more riches. The beggars, maimed, unable to work, ignored by those they were dependent on; while thieves, adept at their trade, stole from rich and poor alike; suffering, all around, for want of comfort. Such was the battleground of the market place.

But the solitary man had returned from a very different battle. A battle fought alone in the searing heat of day and the unforgiving cold of night, without food or shelter, utterly comfortless as he confronted his own destination. In the desert, his only companion, torment.

Now he walked along the shore of the lake empty handed, no wares to sell, no money to buy, with only love and peace to barter with, in the market place of ignorance.

I lowered the rack and turned Damian's coat over, as he was obviously reading the paper for a second time, just as Mick jumped up on his chair, but Damian continued to read, and then turned to me.

"I knew there was something special about her", he began, "but it was difficult to pinpoint. She never said a word you know?" I nodded encouragement and he continued, "Walked to church in all weathers. A very self- contained lady, yet she somehow managed to share and care for others." Damian looked to me for enlightenment.

"I'm afraid I can't help you. We all seem to be, in our own ways, searching for understanding of whom and what she was. This is the reason I really do have to concentrate my time on searching through the papers. Will that be of any use for your meetings?" I asked, looking at the paper he was still holding.

"Yes, if you don't mind I would like a copy. Pity she didn't write any sermons!"

"Well, seeing as you live such a distance, and the rain has stopped, why don't we pop down to the shop now? Then with a little luck you will be able to cycle back in the sunshine."

He managed to perch his bike precariously in the car and we drove down to the village. Having copied the papers, Damian put his hand into his pocket to pay but hesitated and looked at me, so I paid and we left. He returned to the car, got in and shut the door. I got in and he asked me to shut my door.

All was explained when he produced Mick from his pocket. I looked round the car and found a take-away drinks cup, popped Mick in and put the lid on, as Damian explained that he really must repair the lining of his jacket. Having wrestled his bike out of the car, Damian thanked me and cycled off. I drove back explaining to Mick that humans had standards of etiquette and he would definitely not endear himself to folk, by rifling through their pockets in search of lunch. He had been lucky this time.

Chapter Twenty-Four

Humankind has always mistaken freedom for control; the more control they have the more free they will be, but this has never proved the case; because while you live under the illusion that you are in control, freedom can but look on from afar. For what can anybody control with any certainty, except the way they react to each situation they encounter at the moment it occurs. Thus, all our planning for the future is futile; for we plan for a future we cannot predict, and base our plans in the present; plans that are thrown into confusion by any number of incidents outside our control and we have to plan again.

If we stop and think of the things we plan for, and are honest, will we not conclude that most of our plans are grounded in fear; because are we not planning in an attempt to avoid catastrophes in the future, and as we have already seen, the future is as unpredictable to us, as our plans are insecure.

How can we say we have freedom if we constantly plan in an attempt to alleviate our fears? So, the only freedom we have while we are in control is that of making mistakes, for which we will have to pay the consequences, living with anxiety, regret and fear; burdens that become ever heavier to bear. Freedom, if perceived as being able to control our own lives unaided and without hindrance, will always prove elusive. Freedom, if searched for in materialism, power or hedonism, can but look on with tear stained eyes but never reveal itself, as it will not link arms with these to be usurped by man's control. Freedom only has positive outcomes; man's control always leads to torment in all of its guises.

Freedom refuses to be grasped or possessed; it will not coerce or control, nor can it be controlled, for by its very essence it is truly free. Freedom is a hidden treasure, but unlike other treasures it is not to be searched for with maps or by arduous journeys; for we already have access to it, and rather than search for it, all freedom desires is that we approach it in sincerity, with a desire to understand what it has to offer. Then freedom will welcome you; rejoice that you have found it; dry its tears, and unselfishly, patiently and gently, replace your flawed control with its perfect love. For my friend, you will have entered into true freedom, which cannot be attained by human efforts, but is a gift, given freely in love and which will banish your fears.

"You're truly free aren't you Mick, living in the present, one day at a time, not a care in the world. You don't worry about tomorrow or make plans; in fact you don't worry about anything, yet you get along alright don't you? Maybe you have a lot to teach us all." Mick was not taking the least bit of notice, well why should he. He didn't know the meaning of 'care', and took 'freedom' as a norm. But 'come on' I told myself, a mouse is a mouse; but nevertheless is all our care and worry worth the pain? Mick didn't worry where he was going to sleep, and always found something never went hungry.

Were these papers going to lead me anywhere? Maybe I should have locked the bothy up when I had first arrived, and left. Why was I still here? It wasn't necessary, I didn't have to find Avylis, and even if I did, and it seemed increasingly doubtful, what then? What if I did find her? I took the pile of papers I'd already read and settled in front of the fire with a cup of coffee, to try and piece them together.

Mick, who apparently was fearless now, was sitting on the arm of the chair. "What would you do Mick?" Mick just twitched his whiskers and I was about to give him some chocolate when I realised I didn't have any and the cheese was long gone. All I had was half a packet of biscuits so we would share those, I would have to go into the village tomorrow, the oil was low, there was no coal and a visit to the Y.H.A. for a shower would not go amiss.

I threw a log, from the dwindling pile and looked around at the ever-thickening layer of coal dust; the place needed a good clean, but I walked away from it on an impulse to go to the café.

~ ~ ~

Eileen must have seen my car pull up as there was a pot of tea waiting for me. After thanking her and ordering a 'toastie', Eileen had disappeared into the kitchen, and I went over to look at the picture of the lady.

"Speak to me," I whispered, "am I supposed to make any sense of the papers I've found?"

My question remained unanswered but my anxiety was calmed as I looked at her, and in that instant knew there was now only one question to be answered; and it did not rely on finding Avylis, for she had left me all I needed, and her eyes urged me on to find the answer.

"Here we are, now you be careful the plate's hot, mind, I'll just get you some cutlery," Eileen said, placing the plate on the table, and instantly returning with cutlery. "I've put you a few chips on the side," she said, "you're losing weight, do you know that? If you stay much longer we'll be searching for a shadow. You just remember there's always a meal here for you," and with that, and a severe look, she returned to the kitchen, only to return seconds later. "Nearly forgot," she said, " Mrs. Bea told me to tell you, if I saw you, that you're welcome to lunch after church tomorrow. She says you're getting thin and need feeding up. So we can't both be wrong."

"Thanks for the 'toastie' and chips," I said, "and for the

concern. I suppose I have been too engrossed with what I've been doing and simply forgotten to eat. But I promise you I will."

"Good. Stop us all worrying about you." she said winking, as she went to clear tables.

I finished my meal and after thanking Eileen, returned to the bothy.

Chapter Twenty-Five

Picked up, thrown down and spun around in the whirlwind of my mind. Each day I'm flung round faster and end up further away, always searching for myself. But wait - I'm here - why search for me?

My friend found me in the storm and talked to me about patience, peace and stillness, and I listened for a while. But impatient was I with the slow, steady pace and rushed on ahead. But wait-where was I going - and now no- one to show the way.

My guide had sat quietly for six months until I returned, tired, weary and exhausted. "Sit down my friend," he said, "and listen further. "I only go one way, but there are countless others. I sit and watch as most take those other routes and it breaks my heart. Some pass me on the way, and a few stop to talk, but most rush off they know not where.

My friend told me he was at the eye of the storm, where it was peaceful and quiet. "Well," said I, "come and rescue me."
He told me he couldn't leave, because if he did he couldn't guide me; "For," said he, "if I leave here and enter the whirlwind, what good would it do, I'd be just as lost as you. Walk tall my friend, walk fearless, and just keep your eye on me. I will guide you through."

"I can't do it," said I. "I've tried, and failed so many times. I've broken all the promises I made to you. I no longer have the strength; and yet the desire to come with you remains, it is all I want, for you are all I need. But I know I cannot do it on my own and there is no help; and the more I fail the more hopeless it seems. I've grown so tired and despondent."

"Well," he said, "Stay where you are and rest awhile; I will keep you safe while you sleep. Then when you wake, decide if you want to come, because I cannot walk for you. Yet I know we will meet in the eye of the storm, and then when the world rages around in its temper, impatience and noise, stay where you are, my friend, in the eye of the storm. From there you can lend a helping hand; but leave the eye of the storm and you're in an alien land"

I looked for Mick, got up and walked around, but he was nowhere to be seen; so I made a cup of tea, and sat in front of the fire. Ten minutes or so later I hadn't moved, but knew I, wasn't going to find the answers gazing at the fire, and reluctantly returned to the table.

Dearest Friend

For several weeks I tried to keep close to you. I walked and talked with you, but I am so weak and miserable in my love. I often get busy and preoccupied, and during these periods it is not the things that I feel I must do that get shelved, I go on ahead and do those. What does get put to one side, either through tiredness or lack of time, is being with you.

I have grown utterly dependent on your unfailingly love; and tonight I fully realised where I would be without you. How selfish I am; what an ungrateful, miserable wretch I am.

If you did stop loving me then I would indeed have all the rest of my life, living in misery, grief and worse, to reflect on the joy and hope I had lived in while engulfed in your love, and bitterly regretting my selfishness; but alas, all too late for I would have lost your love forever.

But I believe that unless I reject your love, tell you I no longer want it, you will always love me, even though I do take you for granted. You know me better than I know myself, and you also know what is in my heart, despite the fact that at present it may be misguided most of the time. Please forgive me and help me.

Thank you for reading this and not returning it to sender unopened!

"Not returning it unopened?" I muttered, "Return to where? "Oh, Mick," I sighed, grateful for his return, "where does one return a letter to with no address on? Not even an envelope to give a clue or even a postmark. Not even a name. And if it couldn't be returned, she would not even know if it had arrived, that is if she wrote it; but if she received it... and why weren't any of these letters signed?"

Mentally weary, not making any headway, I questioned why I was pursuing my course of action when I constantly ran into brick walls; yet I felt driven on. One could say I was fighting a lone battle on all fronts, with very little artillery, against a phantom force for an unknown cause. Little wonder Eileen said I had lost weight; for nearly three weeks I had sawn and chopped wood, shivered for long periods, walked, not knowing how many miles, just thinking, and all this with remarkably little sustenance. Mick had fared much better on his choc and cheese. Yet I knew that I would continue, for there was now only one question I needed answered and it was crucial, not only regarding Avylis, but for my entire life.

Chapter Twenty-Six

I woke early and heard the birds singing _ or maybe they were complaining – got up and went to the door to negotiate with them. I apologised that they would have to wait but reassured them I was on my way for their supplies and would give them double rations for 'brunch' when I returned. That done, I went indoors and used the last two pieces of bread to make a sandwich–how selfish can one be - and a mug of tea.

Collecting my dirty clothes together and ensuring that Mick had no intention of using his 'free travel pass', I set off for the Y.H.A., skidding erratically down the icy track. As I left the village, I was driving towards an ever moving archway; each colour of the rainbow was identifiable; one end rested on farmland, lighting up the grass by a white farmhouse; the other dipped down over the river; and entranced I almost dipped into the roadside ditch. Pulling onto the verge I stopped to look, in safety.

Given that I was in the warmth of the car, the drive was a delight. I followed the rainbow, painted across a light blue sky, against which small white clouds drifted lazily. The sun illuminated the countryside in its most resplendent colours; snow capped mountains lay in shadows; rivers splashed under small bridges; sheep quietly grazed on the hillsides. I passed by picturesque cottages in small villages, the spires of churches and whitewashed inns, eventually arriving at the natural stone building, which was now the Y.H.A.

I showered and dressed, including donning on my waterproof trousers, hopefully to protect me from my previous forest walk calamity, and collected my clean clothes from the laundry room. After leaving the usual donation I was on my way.

The car park leading to the walks in the forest was empty, and I managed to negotiate the trail this time, without mishap, returning clean, uninjured, and dry. Things were improving.

As I was clean and respectable, and recalling Eileen's admonishment I glanced at the clock on the dashboard and parked outside the "Malt Bottle," three minutes before they stopped serving lunch and had a bowl of asparagus soup and a ham and pineapple sandwich, surely that would keep me in Eileen's good books. Even so, I knew she was right, for my jeans, which usually demanded great determination on my part to zip them up, had succumbed remarkably easily today. Driving back, listening to the radio, under near clear blue skies, my despondency lifted.

Chapter Twenty-Seven

I woke to a chilly morning, lit the fire which I'd set the night before, filled the cauldron for a wash and put water for a drink on the swivel. Large snowflakes fluttered past the window, and had already covered the ground. The sun was rising between the trees as I went out to feed the birds and saw a figure standing looking at the river.

"Good morning," I said. "It's a cold morning for a walk." The figure turned, and I faced an elderly man, dressed in an old fashioned raincoat, far too large for him, wearing wellingtons, and leaning on a walking stick.

"Good morning," he said quietly, smiling.

"I'm just making a cup of tea, would you like one?" I offered. He looked at me for some time. It was a look I was becoming well accustomed to, the same look the children's mother and Mrs. Bea showed when they came here.

"Has it changed since you were last here?" I asked. The man eyed me carefully and then looked up at the bothy, his eyes on the roof.

"I don't quite know why but most folk that come here say it's changed, but I wouldn't know as I have only been here a few weeks," I explained. He looked directly at me, through watery blue eyes, smiled again but made no reply.

"Would you like that cup of tea now? I asked.

"Thank you, it is very kind of you, but I really must be going." He gave a whistle and a little black and white dog raced to his side, and together they walked slowly back down the track, impossible as it seemed, the man looked familiar.

Needing to get a move on if I wanted breakfast before church, I stoked the fire up, then hurriedly delved in my shopping bag from yesterday, locating the small packet of chocolate drops, and left a few for Mick.

"Good morning," Eileen greeted me, "you having breakfast?"

"A quick bacon sandwich please, I'm running late for church."

"Won't be a tick. We don't want you late now, do we?"

Gilbert was just finishing his breakfast, and sighed with satisfaction.

"Good morning," he said, "how are you managing? It's been bitterly cold lately, are you warm enough staying where you are?"

"I've honed my skills as a lumberjack," I replied, demonstrating the fact by clenching my fist and accentuating my biceps, "bought more coal yesterday, and Eileen feeds me well," I reassured him.

Gilbert smiled. "Yes, but even so—"

"Funny thing happened this morning," I interrupted, "there was an elderly man stood outside the bothy, looking at the river. I offered him a drink but he refused, said he had to go. What would he be doing up there on such a cold morning?"

"Cane walking stick, twill cap and little terrier?" he asked.

"Yes." I said waiting for identification, as Eileen brought my breakfast.

Gilbert, wiped his chin on his napkin and folding his paper said, "I'm sorry, but will you please excuse me, Ken has kindly offered me a lift and I mustn't keep him waiting. Pleased to see you again."

"Yes, of course, I must hurry too," I replied looking at the café clock, as I took a firm hold of one half of my double-decker sandwich before the bacon, peering out from all edges, found an escape route and fled to freedom.

~ ~ ~

I parked on the verge outside the Church as every available parking place was taken. The interior of the church was cheerfully decorated with flowers, and the organist, back from holiday, looked in the mirror to his side and stopped playing as the minister entered.

"This is a very special day for two members of our congregation," the minister began. "It is my pleasure to publish the banns of marriage between Mr. Charles Baillie of this Parish and Miss Pamela Quinn, also of this Parish. This is the first time of asking. If there is any impediment you are to declare it." Silence reigned for an interminable time, as if the minister was waiting for some brave soul to voice whatever it was that he was aware of; then deciding that as only he knew, then that was all right.

"We begin our service with hymn number forty-nine." The organist came in on cue, as the congregation stood and sang with gusto; 'To God be the glory, great things he hath done', at which I wondered if the proposed marriage had indeed depended on a little divine intervention. I glanced down to my hymn book, and wondered if, 'Frances J. Van Alstyne 1870' would have approved.

At the close of the service I remained in my pew listening to the organist playing a familiar hymn tune, pondering on the words.

Chapter Twenty-Eight

The minister had already arrived at Mrs. Bea's when I got there, and we sat down to a meal of roast beef with all the trimmings, including our hostess's homemade horseradish sauce, which was chunky and delicious.

"Well," said Mrs. Bea, as she filled three dishes with rhubarb crumble and placed the custard next to the minister, "they finally made it, young Charlie and Pam, then?"

"They did indeed. Finally," replied the minister.

"It doesn't seem any time at all since we all despaired of the boy making anything of his life," Mrs. Bea commented. The minister nodded in agreement.

"He's a lucky young man, Pam's a real nice lass," the minister said.

"She certainly had a good effect on him, calmed him down no end," agreed Mrs. Bea, "and how are you, my dear?"

"All the better for a delicious meal, thank you".

"So what have you been doing with yourself?" asked Mrs. Bea.

I explained about the man I had seen earlier and that somehow he seemed familiar, but knew I must be mistaken; and went on to relate my brief conversation with Gilbert.

The minister suggested it may have been Owen, looking to Mrs. Bea for confirmation. She pursed her lips and said, "Certainly sounds like him." She picked up her handbag and took out a diary. "Yes," she said, "that would be Owen."

"Well in that case," said the minister, "you probably would see the similarity."

"I would?"

"Yes. Do you remember George, your opposition at the debate?
"Er... yes."

"Well Owen is his brother."

"Really, but he looks much older,".

"Twins," said Mrs. Bea.

"Twins. Amazing! He looks so much older and much slimmer build."

"He comes down every year to visit his wife's grave up the valley." Mrs. Bea shook her head, her eyes a mixture of sadness and seemingly hopelessness for Owen. "He then catches the post-bus and visits the farm, but I doubt he'll manage it for much longer, frailer each year, such a shame." Mrs. Bea smiled weakly, "Can't alter the past...," and busied herself pouring tea for us all.

I looked at the minister who added, "Very sad state of affairs, made worse after his wife's death."

"The farm?" I queried.

"Yes, where you are now," the minister explained, "that's the farm....or was the farm."

"But why should he go up there, and in such cold weather?" I asked, as Mrs. Bea removed the empty plates from the table, refilled the teapot, and after she had placed a brightly coloured knitted tea cosy on it, looked at me.

"You see my, dear, Owen used to work the farm with his brother, until George's cattle were struck down with Bovine T.B. Owen gave George most of his savings to restock his farm."

"But surely it affected them both?"

"Yes and no. When their father retired he allowed his sons to continue to work the land, rent free, but he remained the owner." Mrs. Bea paused and the minister continued the story.

"Apparently the boys never got along, always arguing, and their father, a gentle man content just to work and make his way, could never understand their materialistic nature, especially that of George. But truth be known, it seems, they were really just as bad as each other in the earlier days. It was Owen that mellowed with time, but never, it would appear, George."

The minister poured himself another cup of tea, leaving Mrs.

Bea, with a look to the heavens, to replace the tea cosy.

"Well, if they were so antagonistic towards each other why did Owen give George the money?" I asked.

"He had no choice," said Mrs. Bea. "Their father, knowing what his sons were like, divided the farm into two. George reared cattle, Owen sheep. The reason Owen had to help George was that their father had stipulated that the *whole* of the land was farmed by the boys, or he would sell the lot. I don't think he trusted either not to swindle the other. It was probably the only way he could ensure they both had a livelihood. So you see if George had gone under he would have taken Owen with him."

"What happened then?"

"George took the money, used it to go into the building trade, and has done very well for himself, leaving Owen to sell his sheep, which left him without the only job he had ever known and no income."

"He never repaid the money?" I asked although having seen Owen the answer was obvious.

"From what I hear, he could have done several times over...but no," Mrs. Bea said.

"But why does he come here, to the farm, and in such cold weather when he quite clearly isn't well and very frail?"

Mrs. Bea provided the answer. "It's his wife's anniversary today."

"But it must be so painful for him." I said

"In a way, yes there is no denying it," the minister said, as Mrs. Bea attended to the fire, "but also remember he spent many happy hours on the farm with his wife, at times living in the very bothy you are in now, looking after the sheep, especially in the lambing season." My heart sank. I looked at my teacup. What had I done? If, as Mrs. Bea had said, it may be the last time Owen would be able to come. Oh! What damage had I done? I felt a gentle hand on my shoulder, and looked up to see Mrs. Bea's gentle eyes.

"Now don't you go upsetting yourself, my dear, you weren't to know."

"But...." I started.

"I'm sure Owen wouldn't have been upset," the minister said. "On the contrary he would, very likely, be delighted to see the place lived in and alive again, much better than seeing it desolate and falling apart." Mrs. Bea nodded at the minister's remarks.

"Now," said Mrs. Bea, looking at the minister, "I believe you said you were preaching this evening?"

"Indeed I am."

"I think I will be on my way also, and walk my lunch off," I said realising that Mrs. Bea may be in need of a nap; but I knew I wouldn't be walking, I had other things to do.

At any other time during my stay here I would have been grateful for the potted history of the farm, but if there was anything to be gleaned from it, it would have to wait.

Chapter Twenty-Nine

I tentatively thought it may be possible to unravel the mystery, but hadn't I thought that several times before. First when the villagers had been prepared to talk to me about Avylis; finding the papers; Mrs. Bea providing proof of Avylis's writing; all of which had just led to further questions, but this was a totally different matter, and if this was the answer...

I watched Mick scrambling up the table leg and settle down to nibble on a piece of orange rind. "Oh, I don't know, Mick, the only answer I can find is..." I hesitated not wanting to voice it, " and yet, in a way it is plausible; and, if I am right, it has been staring me in the face all the time. Have I just been too blind to see it?" Or, I thought, did I simply *not want* to see it I watched Mick eating the orange. "One advantage you have, my little furry friend, is you'll eat absolutely anything, you're not exactly choosey."

Sooner, rather than later, I had to move on, get out of here; talking to a mouse can't be good for me! Nevertheless, I continued.

"Well let's try and make some sense of it all: She brought ' a kind of peace... had nothing but was content... seemed to want to be alone.... never spoke or chose not to... answered with her eyes... and the minister had affirmed that 'she had no fear, and a deep understanding of others.' Her picture is in the café, Mrs. Bea's cottage, and I suspect many other places around the village; and that picture told, and held all the answers, of this I am sure. Oh! If only I could meet her just for ten minutes Mick. And yet if she never spoke, in a way I have already met her in the picture, if I could but read her eyes."

~ ~ ~

The wind, which had been rising steadily, was now accompanied by a torrential downpour. The sky looked ominous, as thunderous black and sickly yellow clouds pounded across the heavens, blocking out the daylight, creating a fearful noise, as the wind lashed the rain unmercifully. Within minutes the ground was flooded, the water being whipped into wavelets as it ran down the track. Daylight was provided by a flash of yellow lightning, followed by a crash of thunder, then darkness again. I watched through the waterfall that rushed off the roof down the window, as the mirage of skeletal trees swayed crazily in the eerie light. It was the perfect setting for a horror film; a setting so often simulated by film-makers, was being enacted in reality outside my window. Turning away from the scene, I felt cold, threw a shovel of coal on the fire and lit the oil lamp. What would be would be, there was nothing I could do, and so, with a cup of coffee, I went back to the papers and read through my notes on the writings.

... for now I had a friend, a companion with whom to travel.

... deep within me, there is a yearning-a void- that only you can fill.

... yet in my heart I know that I am, at least in your eyes, worth the heartache I cause you.

Trust me, you are safe. You may be unaware of it; you may not understand it; you may not believe it; you may refuse it... and yet. I love you, and there is nothing you can do to alter that.

Well, if the last item was the lover's response, it couldn't have been more emphatic.

Chapter Thirty

There was little doubt about it; all I had read so far was a dialogue between a lover who seemed to have watched, listened and grown to understand every fibre of their beloved, who apparently lacked any such insight. Initially the beloved had accepted the lover without question, gaining confidence in newfound joy, freedom and security, which the lover offered. It was only when the beloved started to question the love they received that feelings of inadequacy fear and self-loathing materialised. Why? And which part did Avylis play - lover or beloved?

Was the letter I had found in the shirt pocket on my arrival here the answer, even the reason why she left? If so, my theory may be right, but even Mick was not to be privy to my thoughts, because I lacked the courage to voice them. Fresh air, albeit icy, nourishment and company were required, in order to rein in my thoughts, which had begun to travel a course I was unwilling to follow.

~ ~ ~

Eileen gave me a stern look as I unconsciously pulled at the waistband of my jeans on entering the café, to be greeted by, "We will be after getting you a pair of braces soon."

Smiling I ordered lunch, and Eileen disappeared into the kitchen.

I stared at the picture of the lady, seeking in her eyes, that inner peace, which allowed her to live contentedly with the bare necessities. It was a peace that conveyed itself to others without a single word. A peace that brought response from others, and once received, it seemed, never to be forgotten. But it was more, a fearless unshakeable peace, for she had left the village frail and ill, walking alone. Avylis had never demanded anything of the villagers yet had received from them gracefully, and in return had seemingly brought them the peace that only love can give. It was impossible to imagine that the face I looked upon had suffered a moment's anxiety; but such character as it showed was not the result of a life lived on calm waters; no, the signs of many a rough passage were clearly etched into the face, but the eyes belied the fact; she had somehow weathered the storms. I gazed at her and she gazed back, refusing to speak. When I had first looked at the picture her eyes had demanded my attention, but now they asked a fearful question!

"Here we are, now come and get it while it's hot. It's freezing today, there's no mistake." I turned from the picture in response to Eileen and walked silently to the table.

"The lady certainly seems to fascinate you... hardly surprising, still, I don't see what is to be gained by just staring at her picture. Have you found out anything about her yet? You surely can't stay in that place much longer, the winters here can be cruel, and that place is hardly... and in any case you seem incapable of looking after yourself... how long have you been here... only a few weeks and your clothes are falling off your back... and have you anything suitable to wear if you do stay, something warm... have you any idea how concerned we are about you? Of course others are too polite to interfere, and I've probably said far too much, but somebody had to," Eileen paused, "now eat your food while it's hot." After the last word of this epistle, my hands flew to my cutlery, for this was not a polite invitation but a command; and at least while I was eating it gave me time to cobble some defence of myself together.

I had read about distress, struggles, desires, freedom, forgiveness, hope and joy; of love, patience and understanding, all, it would seem, in abundance, flowing freely from an inexhaustible source, the lover; but now I had good reason to believe Avylis was the beloved.

Lost in thought, I started as a dish of apple pie with steaming custard was placed in front of me.

Looking up I thanked Eileen, who looked at me shaking her head and saying. "What are we going to do with you?"

"Tell you what," I said, "I'll take two of your pasties and a piece of chocolate cake for my dinner."

"That is all you are going to have? It is *bitterly... cold... weather*, just in case you hadn't noticed. Folk need *hot... nourishing... food* in winter, not a *snack* now and again! At this rate the lady is going to be the death of you. Do you want to lay that at her door?"

"I've got some soup to go with it. And fruit. And a bag of nuts," I rallied.

"Well, at least the soup will be hot I suppose. By the way, I went to the market yesterday, got something for you." She went into the kitchen and returned with a bag. "Thought of you, well how couldn't I when I saw this."

It was a hot water bottle.

"Thanks very much indeed, I had intended buying one." I said sounding apologetically.

"Maybe, but *when* exactly? No use of thinking about it when you've frozen to death, won't be any use to you in your coffin now will it?"

"It would keep the worms warm." I suggested.

Eileen sighed, "I'll go and top your tea up. You're a hopeless case, you know that?"

Chapter Thirty-One

The wind howled, visiting every conceivable crevice, never missing a single corner, whipping up everything in its path and hurling all recklessly high into the air. Young trees bent under the barrage, bowed into humiliation as the wind gained strength; but older trees stood firm and the river defied the storm flowing seemingly undisturbed, until defeated, the wind died down.

Mick ran across the floor to the far corner of the room and stopped.

"Where've you been little fella? Not seen you for some time. Want some choc?" It occurred to me that I wouldn't have been in the least surprised if Mick had answered... but he didn't.

The little room insisted on a thicker layer of smoke and coal dust, while the windows defied the meagre warmth provided by the fire and remained clothed with frost and icicles. Having given up the fight, I ignored both, stoked up the stove and took my tea and my thoughts back to the table.

"Tell me Mick, am I missing something? Here we have someone who rescued Avylis from despair, demanding nothing of her, accepting her as she was; and initially, she enjoyed her new-found friend, and all was well. It seemed it was only when she questioned her lover that she again slipped into despair... why? Why question? How could such love lead to despair? Avylis admits she took it all for granted. Did she feel guilty? Maybe she felt unworthy of such love; after all she denounced herself as 'a miserable wretch'. Or was it that she tried to respond but...." I sighed before taking another track.

"Normally two lovers care for each other, give and take. Yes?

But what if Avylis had concluded that this was all beyond her, all her efforts it seemed led to only more torment and suffering?"

I watched Mick who was sitting on the pile of, as yet, unread papers, which I had explained, several times, were difficult enough to read without him scrambling all over them, nibbling them, and worse; but right now I needed him there.

"What would I do Mick, if I had the perfect companion; someone who cared enough to provide freedom, security, and who always forgave me? Let's face it, Mick, Avylis had it all - and maybe - yes maybe, *that* was the problem; for if I had such a lover surely I would want to respond, but could I? Would *I* be prepared to be ignored, misunderstood or denied? Could I offer complete freedom, wait patiently, and then welcome them back? In short Mick, could I love unconditionally? Can anyone love unconditionally? Should anyone love unconditionally?"

Mick circled the papers and scrambled off the table. If he had the answers he wasn't saying, but I had to admit, for a mouse his attention span was phenomenal.

Papers I had yet to read, the familiar hymn, and the unspoken question asked by Avylis this morning needed my attention, but I had ignored all, quite simply out of fear. From the moment of crossing the threshold of the bothy I had been on a quest to find the truth about my benefactor; but did I really want the truth, could I endure the truth? I knew that I had come very close to it, so close that one more step could seal my fate. I could leave now and always be unsure, or stay, and be certain. There was little choice either way, live with the unknown, or live with the knowledge. The former would haunt me; the latter could destroy me. Either way Avylis had changed my life forever.

I picked up the next unread sheet to read in bed.

The contours of the hills and fields in the background, against the pale grey sky, have their own unique textures and colours. The hills circle the water, gently looking down in silent protection. The expanse of water, warmed and lit by the sun, glides effortlessly in the breeze, like a huge galaxy of stars. Birds float above, no concerns have they. The burly motorcyclist dismounts, and walks to the empty bench beside the water. We all need peace, and on that bench sits my friend, patiently waiting for company.

Trees in the foreground stand perfectly still; content with the slow daily process of letting their roots slowly transform the skeleton branches into life. But, the trees have no cares, they know that just being there, staying still, they will grow and flourish with leaves, blossom and berries. Then, they will welcome birds as daily visitors, or provide a home for summer. A myriad of insects will visit and the trees will give freely of their bounty until all are satisfied. The leaves, berries and blossoms will fall, to be welcomed by the earth for carpeting and nurture. Then the trees will rest, in the knowledge that they will flourish again in season

The little bench, now empty, but my friend waits, until someone sees him there and goes to share the silence; the silence of love and complete understanding. So I went and sat on the bench, saying not a word. No need to question, why or how, enough to know it was, is, and will be.

Chapter Thirty-Two

Having donned three sweaters, anorak, woolly hat and two pairs of gloves I ventured out to find a broken tree branch with quiet optimism after the winds of yesterday, and found one easily. What I had forgotten was that there had also been torrential rain, and it took more patience than I am normally endowed with, and all my strength to part it from the tree, but there was little choice unless Eileen's prediction of my demise was to be fulfilled. All that was left was half a bucket of coal to keep the fire going overnight, and four small logs. Whatever happened tomorrow I must get some more coal, bird food, chocolate and dry logs, as the ones I had just chopped,being wet would smoke and spit.

The mystery of Avylis invaded my thoughts. It needed to be solved. She must have been a tough lady, for I had only been here a matter of weeks. She had lived here for two years and would have endured two, maybe three winters. The luxury of buying logs and coal for Avylis, would I am sure, have been out of the question; and a hot water bottle, she would probably have regarded as an unnecessary luxury. As for a shower and laundry facilities well... the simple truth was, that as far as anyone knew, she only had five pounds which was recycled regularly, so she managed on what she had, and somehow did so cheerfully. The only other living creature I knew that would have understood her was Mick, and even he had his little luxuries.

The longer I stayed the more I realised what a remarkable lady Avylis was. I certainly would not have lasted long having to boil all the water to wash my clothes, chop all the wood, cook all my food in the bothy, and could I have coped with the loneliness?

I returned to my task.

> *I awoke to the sun rolling down the hills awakening the forest*
> *on its travels, before spilling the evening stars into the river.*
> *The dense forest climbed up the hillside, gradually thinning*
> *until just a crooked finger reached out to the top and beyond.*
> *It called me to follow, to a place where I could see the*
> *panoramic view, yet knew it was beyond my capabilities; but,*
> *'Climb as far as you are able.'*
> *I started on an ill defined track which was soon lost; but I had*
> *to climb, and continued blindly until the track reappeared,*
> *and eventually reached a clearing where I could rest... and*
> *stay? But...*
> *'Look around my friend, is this the view you seek?'*
> *My vista was narrow, closed in by trees.*
> *I climbed again in the hope that at the next turn the track*
> *would level, yet always met by another upward climb. When*
> *I considered turning back, the restraining hand of the wind*
> *lay gently on my back, and breathed encouragement;*
> *'To descend is hazardous, and in time you will have to climb*
> *again, you know that.'*
> *I trudged on until I stood at the top, and looked at the*
> *panoramic view before me, and like giving birth, the fear,*
> *anguish, exhaustion and pain expire into the glorious strength*
> *of joy. Now, here I could settle. My body, stretched and torn*
> *with effort, my mind knotted with the threads of anguish, my*
> *heart mocked by loneliness, could all rest, they had nothing*
> *left to give, they had reached their destination.*
> *Then I turned and scanned the skies and the rugged barren*
> *rock of the mountain face called down to me, beckoning*
> *from lofty peaks hidden in the clouds, and I realised that my*
> *journey had only just begun.*
> *I looked across the ridge towards the mountain. There would*
> *surely be water, but no soft bedding provided by grass and*
> *earth, little shade from the sun or shelter from the storm, and*
> *what friends live there, so high? The butterflies and sheep,*

the birds and insects, the frogs and field mice and all the others, will they greet me?

But first I had to cross the ridge, an easy walk with fresh air and clear vistas, rest and renew my strength, and decide what I needed; for the mountain was far too steep to carry all I had, most would have to be left behind, because I could not deny the mountains call to climb above the clouds to the peak.

Another conversation? But weren't they all? Yes, that was it! Not letters, but... but what? Thoughts? Reflections? They could even be meditations. My fears grew, but I had to continue looking through the papers.

> *What are you about to say?*
> *Is it to complain?*
> *Keep quiet.*

> *What are you about to say?*
> *Is it in anger?*
> *Keep quiet.*

> *What are you about to say?*
> *Is it to praise yourself?*
> *Keep quiet.*

> *What are you about to say?*
> *Is it to blame someone?*
> *Keep quiet.*

> *What are you about to say?*
> *Is it to encourage?*
> *Speak quietly.*

> *What are you about to say?*
> *Is it to comfort?*
> *Speak gently.*

I turned the sheet over.

> *Listen*
> *What do you hear?*
> *Difficulties,*
> *Failures,*
> *Anger.*
>
> *Listen,*
> *What do you hear?*
> *Worry,*
> *Fear,*
> *Doubt.*
>
> *Listen,*
> *What do you hear?*
> *Nothing.*
>
> *Listen,*
> *What do you hear?*
> *Calm,*
> *Peace*
> *Silence*
>
> *Listen,*
> *What do you hear?*
> *Forgiveness,*
> *Reassurance,*
> *Compassion.*
>
> *Speak,*
> *What will you say?*

This could explain why Avylis chose not to speak; but how could she listen to her friend whom, for two years at least, she was unable to contact? How did the relationship survive? Maybe it was the reason she chose not to speak; but could anyone live by such a code?

No! No!, No! Stop avoiding the question I admonished myself. Stop deluding yourself, you know who her friend is, have always known; no that was wrong too; you have always known of him through what others have told you. You have learned from others who probably have also heard stories of him, but did they *know* him?

The only person I knew for sure who had searched - searched not through looking, not through asking, not through following some directive, or journeying to where he had once lived but meeting with him - listening and talking to him - and yes - writing to him.

That was the essence of the peace that shone out of Avylis's eyes. True, the face was scarred with pain, but that wasn't what had captivated me as I had looked at her picture, no it was her eyes that shone out from the pain surrounding them. It was the light of her eyes that threw the torment around them into shadow. Hadn't she written about 'the eye of the storm'?

Chapter Thirty-Three

Entering the church, knowing that the regular minister was away, and wondering who would take the service, I saw Hannah, looking across to me and I walked over to say 'Hello' and sat in their pew. Hannah was asking her mother, "Can I sit next to her?"

Mother, asked if I would mind and moved Hannah next to Kate. "But I want to sit next to you as well mummy," cried Hannah. Kate, with obvious clear sighted-ness, looked to heaven, moved to the other side of me and Hannah settled down, as I turned to Kate and whispered, "You're a good girl, Kate."

Damian walked out of the vestry, and I waited in anticipation. The service proceeded with the intimations and a hymn throughout which Hannah, tongue waggling between clenched lips concentrated on putting a coin into the paw of Boo, who in turn now dropped it into the collection box, and Boo was rewarded as Hannah whispered, "You're a good boy, Boo."

The other children left during the following hymn for their own activities, but Hannah decided to stay, and kept Kate by her side.

The apologetic nervous young curate, who constantly snacked on his fingernails, and had spoken at the tempo of an express train, took the lectern, bowed his head, then looked directly at the congregation and said clearly and slowly. "Blessed are the poor in spirit. What are we to glean from this?"

He looked at the congregation for a minute in silence; maybe he was expecting the answer. But no, he continued.

Hannah sat still, for about three minutes, then shuffled in her seat, eventually sitting Boo by her side. Having accomplished this she looked at Boo, picked him up and sat him on her knee, facing forward; obviously not satisfied she picked bear up and scrutinised him before turning to look at me.

"It's no use," Hannah, said quietly, with a deep sigh, "I'll *have* to take Boo out."

"Why?"

"He's *bored*, I 'spect he's *too young?*" she whispered.

"Well, I'm sure you're right."

"Will you come too? she asked.

"I think I may be too old," I whispered.

"You're not as old as Miss Will-o-bee," she countered.

"Sunday school is for children!" Kate informed her in such a loud whisper, heads turned, "I'll come with you." Kate took hold of Hannah's hand and walked down the aisle to the door on the left, already being held open.

Nicely done Hannah, I thought, smiling. No one could argue that Hannah had Boo's interest at heart, and she did of course have to accompany her young charge, (not to do so would be irresponsible). Mission accomplished; Hannah had acted responsibly, Boo was relieved from boredom, and Kate had escaped the sermon. Four year-old Hannah was certainly a '*tour de force*'.

On leaving the church I asked Damian if he would mind lending me the copy of his sermon. "Well... er... yes of course. But if you could wait a few minutes."

As Hannah approached the door, I congratulated her on how well-behaved Boo was during the service. "Oh! He's *always* good in church, I *insist* on it!"

"Quite right too," I said seriously, winking at Kate, who looked at her sister and shook her head.

"Thanks for waiting," Damian said, "matter of fact I was hoping to have a word with you."

"Well in that case why don't you let me treat you to lunch tomorrow?" and immediately added, reading Damian's thoughts, "there must be somewhere suitable where you live, save you time and pedal energy?"

"Oh, I really couldn't't'..."

"Course you could," I insisted.

Damian grinned, probably relieved that I wasn't going to inflict the Spartan cuisine of the bothy on him, and said, "Okay, I'll meet you at the 'Horse and Farrier' about midday, they do 'Two for One' Monday lunch."

"Fine, see you there."

~ ~ ~

Sleep evaded me, even though it was a dry, still, night. Pulling on my sweater, I got out of bed, and went to the window. Stars dripped from the sky like a chandelier. I mustered my rations; three slices of bread, a small piece of cheese, (from which the mould could be cut off), an apple and a tin of beans.

All my thoughts seemed to dissolve in the warm glow of the fire. Yes, in such circumstances, with food inside me, warmth in front of me, and all fears behind me, (or temporarily forgotten), I could stay longer. The flames leapt about. There was no phone to ring, no clocks to tick, no fridge to hum, and no traffic noise. I wondered if the average person ever had the opportunity of experiencing complete silence, and could I ever again live without it?

Chapter Thirty-Four

The morning dawned quietly. Trees transformed into frosted glass statues, stood quite still. The sun, unhindered in a pale blue sky, enhanced my view across the hills to the mountains beyond. I crunched through the newly laid carpet of frost to feed the birds and watched as the shadows danced around them. Oblivious of the icy air, I felt extraordinarily privileged.

Back indoors, after breakfast I returned to my task, but was brought to an abrupt halt at the end of the first sheet:

... Will you forsake all else and come?

Lightning seared across the icy surface of my brain, etching the question in deep indelible letters. My head dropped to the table and my tears fell, unhindered, onto the precious papers. I stared into space searching for another explanation, an easier one; then I was engulfed with fear; and then regretted not locking the bothy and leaving on my first visit.

When I had asked Mick, 'had I just been too blind to see the answer', now I acknowledged, what I had known then but denied. No! I couldn't undertake what Avylis asked of me. I wasn't made from the same mould as her. I wasn't strong enough. Not committed enough. It was far beyond me. I was inadequate in every way. I put my head in my hands knowing I was looking for an easy exit, but had travelled onwards eagerly, encouraged by the peace I had seen in her eyes, the peace I yearned for... and had hit the buffers.

The firelight flickered around the room, as my thoughts

ricocheted around my brain. What did I do now? I had tried so hard over the weeks to unravel the mystery of Avylis and now wished it could all be reeled in. What did I do now? The only... escape... no... I could no longer escape, rather an attempt, to stop my mind darting about. I had to get back to some form of normality, calm down, and think clearly.

~ ~ ~

I glanced in the café before entering, there was only Gilbert having breakfast, reading his paper, and a couple of strangers. Eileen looked up from taking an order from the couple and said, "Morning."

Acknowledging her I sat at the corner table. Eileen came over, still scribbling on her pad. "Are you ready..." she began before looking at me, "are you alright?"

I shook my head.

"I'll just get these meals. I'll be back in a tick," she said.

From where I sat, the picture was indecipherable and I looked away from it.

"What on earth is wrong with you?" Eileen asked, with concern.

We stared at one another, as I thought, she won't understand, nobody would understand, and moaned, "I don't know." The words fell out, as we continued to stare at each other.

"Would you like to lie down for a bit, I'll get you a hot water bottle."

I shook my head.

"A hot drink then?" Eileen suggested.

I nodded.

As she went to the kitchen Gilbert folded his paper neatly and walking to the door asked, "Are you all right?"

I nodded.

"Well, if you say so, but look after yourself in this cold weather." I nodded again, and he stared at me for a minute, most ungentlemanly, at least for Gilbert. He crossed to the door, turned and looked at Eileen, who nodded at him, and with a

121

quick glance at me, he opened the door and left.

Eileen placed a mug of steaming tea on the table, informing me that she had put two sugars in it. Wrapping my hands around it, I thanked her, as she turned to thank the couple as they left and went to clear the table. I sipped the tea, carefully, once aware that it may have a tea leaf in it, but was in fact 'whisky on sugar'.

Alone in the café I looked at Avylis and said, "I can't do it."

It may have been a trick of the light but was there a twinkle in her eye? I repeated, "I can't do it." She just stared back as I looked into her eyes. "I haven't got what it takes." I moaned. "You had, but I haven't." Her eyes, filled with understanding and compassion for my plight, looked into mine. It was as if she knew I had no choice. "Where do I start?" I asked. "Give me some help, I can't do this alone" Her look was one of encouragement and strength.

"We'll have to keep an eye on you and no mistake." I turned as Eileen continued, "Can't have you talking to pictures now can we? I'll make a coffee while it's quiet. In the meantime, if you're not convinced by Gilbert or me go look in the mirror."

Obediently I went into the toilets and looked; and realised some explanation, even if it was to be a white lie, was needed. I splashed some hot water on my face and dried it vigorously with the paper hand towel.

"It'll take more than hot water to get your colour back." Eileen stated as I sat down with her.

"Honestly, I do appreciate your concern, and I will admit that I occasionally get pain in my hand. I broke my arm a while back. Normally, it doesn't bother me at all but I suppose it's the cold weather. It would help if I remembered to wear my gloves." I attempted a smile. "I have some tablets for it and usually it goes in a matter of days, but I didn't get much sleep last night." I knew I was talking gibberish, and also knew that Eileen wasn't convinced.

She didn't comment, she just asked, "How long do you intend staying, because it is likely to get much colder?"

"I don't know."

"Well if you want a warm bed for a few nights and some decent food you are welcome to stay. But I can't do it until the weekend as my mother came last night for a few days. Will you at least think about it?"

"That is really kind, but I don't want to trouble you. You're busy enough with the café." I said.

"I'm quite used to visitors, so no need to worry about that. Please think about it. You look ill to me, and a little warmth and comfort will do you no harm whatsoever." Eileen replied, clearly concerned.

"Thank you." I said, feeling even worse that I had lied to her.

"Now then," Eileen said. "I just have a few lunch boxes to make up for the lads. They'll be in shortly, and then I'm going to close early, it's never so busy on Monday—".

"What time is it?" I interrupted.

"Ten past eleven."

"Oh, I'm going to have to rush, promised to meet someone at twelve, nearly forgot. Thank you for your concern I really do appreciate it, and for the coffee." I rose to go.

"No trouble at all and I expect to see you improved by tomorrow."

"I will be. Bye, and thanks. See you tomorrow." I said as I went out the door.

Chapter Thirty-Five

I arrived five minutes late. The little inn was crowded and Damian was settled at the nearest table to the roaring fire.

"I'm really sorry, have you been waiting long?" I asked Damian, taking off my jacket.

"No, I was just in time to 'nick' the best table, it's filled up amazingly fast. How are you today?" he asked, for which I was grateful, as it made a change from others telling me how I felt, but it was to be short lived, as before I could answer he said, "I've got to say I've seen you better. Bit under the weather?"

"A bit, but nothing lunch won't cure," I responded with a smile, and glanced at the menu.

"Well we'd better eat then," Damian said. One thing I had learned during my stay was that if food is placed in front of members of the clergy then there is absolutely no point in trying to penetrate their minds, their stomachs are entirely in control.

"I really enjoyed that," Damian said handing his plate to the waitress, who, from her demeanour, was regretting the 'dog collar' and glanced at me. I just smiled, but yes I agreed. She asked me if I'd finished, looking at the remains of my lunch, and I thanked her as she removed the plate. Damian thankfully made no comment.

I was warming to my companion, who was a cocktail of affability, shyness and uncertainty; all underpinned with a quiet confidence; but the one thing that would always elude him, was any form of vanity. He was that rare specimen who recognised all his own faults, but overlooked those in everybody else.

"You said you wanted a word with me," I said, "usually that means I'm in trouble!" Damian obviously understood.

"Nice to know I'm not the only one. But seriously I wondered if you had any more reflections we could use. The group is enthusiastic, but only two actually submitted their own, and if we are to continue I will need a least two more. I could always, of course, fill the gaps myself." Damian sipped his coffee.

"It will increase your work load so close to Christmas," I said.

"True, but there are several people in the group that do not attend church, so I don't mind, and certainly don't want to discourage them, and shouldn't really be asking you, as you are so busy..." I waited to see if he had simply run out of breath or had actually finished.

"Hey, you do more in a day than I do in a week, I'm not *that* busy," I protested, wondering how long it would take for his enthusiasm to be dampened by the apathy of his flock before adding, "and I do appreciate your predicament; everyone appreciates the meetings but few are prepared to provide the tools for the job. You know, someone once told me that they thought churchgoers regarded it as a form of entertainment; they come and listen and sing, and afterwards use the venue as a social club. I often wonder what would happen if, like the cinema, there was a five pound admission fee."

Damian raised an eyebrow and said, "Oh hang on I wouldn't' go that far," looked down at his coffee, looked up again and said, "But if I'm honest..."

"Don't take too much notice of me, after all what do I know. And in any case as you rightly pointed out I am not quite myself today, but I'm sure I could find a couple," and rashly added, "I'll pop them in your letter box tomorrow."

"Thanks that would be a great help."

"Are you not going to apologise for being a nuisance, tell me I couldn't possibly as I'm far too busy, under the weather and need rest etc. etc." I teased.

Damian just stared at me, and then laughed. "Not this time," he replied. "I'm just grateful."

"Good," I replied smiling, feeling deceitful, knowing that my promise may not be fulfilled but desperate to leave and be alone.

"Now what did you want to pick my brain about?" he asked.

I skipped over this; it didn't matter anymore. "Just to see if I could have a copy of your sermon, as I was otherwise occupied with a teddy bear and a youngster trying to persuade me to go to Sunday school!"

"Of course." He opened his jacket and took it from his inside pocket. "I've got it here."

"Thanks."

"Now if you'll excuse me I must be off, got two funerals tomorrow," Damian concluded.

"Yes, I've things to do too." I said getting up and putting on my jacket, having settled the bill. Damian walked with me to the car and waited until I got in before speaking. "You know, it's nothing to do with me but you look as if you should be in bed."

"I'll be OK thanks, don't worry."

Chapter Thirty-Six

I started the car, pulled away then stopped, not having the faintest idea where I was going. Half an hour later my eyes scanned the familiar scene. Sheep, usually grazing, were huddled together on the hard white ground against the dry-stone wall. Beyond the dark farm buildings, the frozen stream clothed the stepping stones, which led walkers over to the granite fells. : A tractor emerged from beyond the dark buildings, its engine noisily arousing the sheep, setting them off at a run towards the hayrack, bringing the monochrome tableau to life

It was bitterly cold, but I had to think.

I had spent weeks living in a cold stone bothy, with only icy water from the stream, and a mattress on the flagged floor; and on several occasions felt as if there was ice in my joints that cracked in my every movement. I had survived blizzards, downpours, thick frosts, icicles on the wrong side of the windows, and the building being ripped apart; and yes, lost weight, quite a lot; but I had done so cheerfully and enjoyed the peace, but now I knew that peace would not surrender to infatuation, but only true unselfish love. What was that quote, 'to be more desirous to have our curiosity gratified, than to have our conscience directed...' Maybe, but none of this was of my own making. I had no idea that an unknown benefactor was going to enter from the wings of my life and place me centre stage. Avylis had struggled; she had won her private battle at an awful cost, and had been prepared to pay whatever was asked. Am I prepared to pay whatever may be asked of me?

I had come to think, but my mind, used to working within

normal limits of the everyday, was now like the river, it had frozen, needing time to re-adjust, expand and explore new horizons way outside its normal perimeters.

It was past four, the sun had set, taking all of humanity with it, never to rise again; leaving me alone on a dark, cold, desolate, friendless planet, fearful and cold.

The car engine broke the silence and the headlights were the only light to lead me back, but they alone couldn't do it, the indicator on the dashboard demanded more fuel. There was nothing to do but drive and hope, otherwise I would be little more than part of the frozen landscape by morning. Did I care?

Chapter Thirty-Seven

I rolled off the mattress, pulled on a sweater and went to light the fire. The remaining logs would heat enough water for a hot drink and a wash. I hadn't ventured out of the bothy for three days. The facts I hadn't washed during that time, and had eaten little, were irrelevant, but logs and coal were essential. After a quick wash, dressing, and a mug of hot water, (the tea packet was empty), I drove into the next village, not wanting to be drawn into conversation, and got the necessary supplies; then, once again, drove without knowing where.

The sunshine on the pale green grass, snow-capped hills and frost covered trees, no, not even the bird song penetrated my despondent mind. After an hour, maybe two, came across welcoming little inn.

~ ~ ~

With little appetite I ordered a toasted sandwich and waited. The sandwich, served on thick wedges of homemade bread, came on an enormous plate, accompanied by a full salad, crisps, a large helping of coleslaw and garnished with various herbs. Looking up from the plate, over faced at what was on my plate, an elderly gentleman, on the adjacent table smiled at me.

"I only popped in for a snack," I said.

The white haired gentleman explained that he had learned the lesson and now simply had soup and a sweet. His wife, presumably, walked over to join him, stared at me, then at her husband who immediately looked down and fiddled with the condiments. I picked at the food in front of me. The waitress informed me that they were expecting a party of people shortly, so coffee would be served in the adjoining area

Having eased myself into the unaccustomed comfort of a large leather sofa in the far corner, in an attempt to hide myself, my heart sank as I desperately looked round for a leaflet, menu, anything to read as the elderly gentleman who had spoken to me earlier, led by his wife, came and sat on the sofa on the opposite side of the coffee table, despite the fact there were several free tables.

"It is a bitter day—" the gentleman, mouth agape, was interrupted by a glare from his wife, who instructed him not to state the obvious, and to close his mouth if he had nothing constructive to say, which she doubted. Her husband looked down at his coffee.

"Now, what are you doing in these parts?" demanded the lady.

"Oh, just passing through," I said hoping she would take the limited response as a signal that I did not want to talk.

"Yes, but where are you staying?" she continued.

"As I stated, I'm just passing through."

"Yes, you said that, but exactly where from and where to?" She stared at me as if I had committed the gravest offence.

"Sorry, would you please excuse me for a minute?" I asked

"How strange you've only just sat down," she said, as I got up and walked away.

As I saw it, I had three options to avoid the inquisition. Firstly to leave, secondly to be rude and simply sit somewhere else, or thirdly return to my unwelcome company; but, overriding all else, was the fact it was warm and comfortable, so I returned to my instructor on impropriety.

As I approached the table, the inquisitor gave me a wan smile, and before I was seated said, "Now, you were about to tell me where you are staying"

"Was I?" I countered. She glowered defiantly, and then quickly replaced the wan smile. Surely I hadn't left her speechless. No.

"I have lived here for a long time, so you see I know the area and most of the people," she informed me.

While we stared at each other, a quiet voice said, "Oh, I doubt it dear; it was a long time ago."

With one swift pivotal movement of her head, his wife shot a glance that effectively shackled her husband firmly back into place, and then glanced round the restaurant, like a school teacher checking that all her students were paying attention, and indeed they were.

"Now, you were about to tell me, where you were staying." The demand was accompanied by a crumpled smile.

The thin scarlet slash below a small pointed nose led my eye upwards to steely grey slits, underlined with black, and protected under an ominous green shadow. Burning cheeks painted either side completed the picture painted onto the creased scroll. Above was iron grey hair, severely drawn back and manipulated into a tight bun. This was the image facing me as I flicked through the brief facts of the past few weeks, missing out the name of the village; my encounters with the villagers; my legacy; and Avylis's name, merely telling her that I was searching for ' a lady', and the basic facts about Avylis, in the hope I could extricate myself politely

As I concluded the short account, the painted scroll stared at me, then turned to her husband and declared authorititively, "Father David would know."

"Father David?" her husband said, clearly puzzled.

"Father is bound to know," she asserted.

"Is he?" questioned her husband.

"Of course he is," she retorted, as her husband gestured to me that he hadn't a clue who or what his wife was talking about.

"Who is Father David?" I asked. My interrogator and teacher was clearly exasperated, knowing that she had explained quite succinctly once, could not, and would not tolerate those who had not listened.

"Well he does all the burials doesn't he?" she said. This simple statement was delivered as if by a sleuth who had solved the crime while everyone else still floundered after the first clue.

"But we don't know if she is dead," her husband paused before daring to ask, "do we?"

His wife looked at the two imbeciles she had been burdened with, sighed, lifted one hand off the table and with the other hand pointed a long thin crooked finger, lined with blue and tipped with a blood red talon, to the little finger on the other hand. She continued in a slow clear voice, giving no excuse for the person on the highest, remotest tier of the coliseum, not to hear.

"Look at the facts." She began to tick 'the facts' off with her 'bloody' talon. "She was feeble, old and ill; walked away in the dead of winter, in the freezing cold, at night, in the dark, had inadequate clothing, no food, and little money. She was at least forty miles from the nearest hospital, there was no police station, no phone and in any case she couldn't speak. No taxis, public transport, little traffic, and, after she left the village, no habitation. How long would it take for her to fall, suffer hypothermia or lose consciousness due to lack of food? Of course she's dead!" she ended triumphantly.

Following this performance, which admittedly had entertained the clientele, coffees were once again sipped, , staff animated, and conversations resumed. I excused myself.

The manager took payment for my meal, as I enquired if the couple were local. The manager leaned over the bar towards me and whispered, conspiratorially. "She lived here as a child and returned about five years ago. You have just encountered our very own Miss Marple," he said, holding my gaze.

"Surely not," I gently protested, "Miss Marple, as I remember, was quiet and self-effacing."

"You know that, and I know that; but what you have to remember is..." he glanced at the woman in question, "our version merely cut her teeth on Miss Marple; and then..."

"Promoted herself." I anticipated.

The manager, still holding my gaze said, "She's harmless until the uninitiated walk in, as you did this evening, then we all get entertained, it's good for business!"

"You should try Murder Mystery dinners," I whispered.

"Oh! We did but nobody else—"

"Could get a word in," I finished.

"Got it in one."

"And she complained about the script and the plot," I added.

"Absolutely," he said still looking me in the eye. We both looked across at the sleuth.

"And what does your Miss Marple do when the uninitiated don't walk in?" I asked.

"Oh, she reads the papers avidly and solves any murders that may crop up, or if the police actually manage to solve them, or at least think they have, though of course they are quite obviously wrong, you understand." I nodded "Then she skips through the latest "Crimewatch" solving the lot before you could finish your soup."

"I just can't imagine her skipping," I said.

"Bulldozing?"

"Nearer the mark." I agreed. "Actually you maybe could solve the only problem I have right now," I suggested.

"What's that?" he said standing upright again.

"Where exactly am I?

"What do you mean?"

"What do you mean, Ma'am!" I corrected.

"Oh! Don't you start."

"I'm lost," I admitted, "not a clue where I am, and I wasn't about to ask your detective, wouldn't give her the satisfaction."

He gave me directions, adding, "Nice talking to you, take care and don't get lost."

"Enjoyed the chat, and thanks for the directions," I replied, turned at the door and smiled.

He replied with a wink as he said, "See you soon, don't leave it too long."

Chapter Thirty-Eight

My recent encounter at the inn was soon forgotten as I drove the fifty miles back to the bothy, trying desperately to decide what to do next. The only decision reached was to read the remainder of the papers before making a decision; my powers of avoidance over the past few days had been honed to perfection, by my new friend, procrastination.

There was a note pinned to the bothy door, and a carrier bag on the ground. On entering, the cold air sliced through my bones. After lighting the fire I read the note while waiting for the water to boil. *'Sorry I missed you. Eileen.'* The café would be closed so I would make my peace with Eileen tomorrow.

The last tear stained paper still lay on the table. I picked up another.

> *I danced towards the flame of love,*
> *Which bordered the void within me.*
> *Fearless was I, because I knew you were enough.*
> *Then you asked me to place my whole life into your care,*
> *And while I thought you said,*
>
> *Did you ever believe you would leave and travel alone?*
> *See the places you've seen?*
> *Meet the friends you now have?*
> *Find the peace you have found?*
> *That you would listen to me, and learn so much?*
> *And my answer to all was, no.*

Have I not provided for all your needs?
Loved you, forgiven you and been your friend?"
And my answer to all was, yes.
Then he said.
You started your journey saying, I was enough.
Now I ask you: Am I?
You quite rightly believe that there is more, much more.
And you believe me when I tell you,
That for all you have experienced, you have been too easily
satisfied.
But my friend the choice is yours; do you want to come?

I looked around for Mick, needing to voice my thoughts, but I was utterly alone in the silent night with only the firelight, the flickering lamp, and my thoughts. This now had little to do with Avylis; she had made her decision, and that thought brought anger for the first time. Why had Avylis chosen to force *me* into a decision, a decision I thought I'd *already* made, that would turn my life upside down? Why me?

How could I have allowed myself to be drawn into a situation that had nothing to do with me; for tolerating the conditions I had lived in? The solution was to leave, forget all about it and return to some sort of normality, but Avylis hadn't even left me that option. Mick scrambled onto the chair in front of the fire.

"And where were you when I needed you!"

I sat with a mug of tea at the table, unwilling to disturb Mick, the only living company I had, when the whole room was lit up, followed by a crash of thunder, torrential rain, and a rising wind.

"Here we go again," I informed Mick.

Chapter Thirty-Nine

The dry, calm morning greeted me with brilliant sunshine; had the thaw come at last; maybe, as the ground was devoid of any frost and there was only a smattering of snow?

The café was full, for which I was grateful, as Eileen was busy. I crept in, manoeuvring past several rucksacks, and sat down quietly at the small corner table.

"Morning, stranger, be with you in a tick," Eileen looked at me, shook her head and returned to her customers.

My breakfast was served with instructions to 'eat it all'. Meanwhile the rucksacks were repossessed and tables surrounded by chatter and laughter were left littered and silent. I watched the slight figure of Eileen whisk around as she piled dishes, moved chairs, wiped tables and placed condiments and menus swiftly into place. When she had reclaimed neatness and order, she looked across at me. "Coffee?"

I nodded.

"What have you been doing with yourself, thought you'd left?" Eileen asked placing two coffees on the table. "Just look at you." She passed a critical eye over me and my breakfast, now pushed to one side.

"Sorry, I've not been in, had a few things to do," I offered weakly.

"Well one wasn't eating, that's obvious," I drank my coffee, thinking how to change the subject.

"Thanks for leaving the note," I said, and was ignored.

"I spend two weeks getting an ounce of weight back on your bones and in three days....

"I really am sorry but I needed time to think; to decide what to do." Eileen picked her coffee cup up and then replaced it on the saucer.

"Thinking... for three days?" she mused.

"To be honest, for most of the time I've just driven around."

"Where did you get to?" she asked.

"Haven't a clue, yesterday I had to ask for directions back."

Eileen inhaled deeply, and sighed, "So did three days of thinking..." she stressed the last word, "do any good?"

"Not a lot. I already knew the answer."

"Mmm."

"I suppose I was really trying to come to terms with the answer," I said thoughtfully.

Eileen was struggling, which was hardly surprising for anyone with such a practical straightforward view of life, unhindered with riddles and enigmas. "Anything I can help with?" she offered.

"Unfortunately not, I wish someone could."

Eileen smiled, "Another coffee?"

"Never say no to a coffee. Thanks."

She disappeared into the kitchen. The phone rang, but if she heard, chose to ignore it. The café looked different, and at first it was difficult to know why, until I saw that the picture of Avylis had been taken down; it didn't matter.

"Here we are," said Eileen, walking over with fresh coffees.

"Where are the pictures and teapots?" I asked.

"My mother took them down and cleaned them, ready to go back when I've painted."

"Do you do it?"

"If I have to, but the boys help at weekend if they can, depends on the weather."

"The weather?"

"Yes. Last time they had their hands full. Three years ago it was, we had heavy snows which drifted, and the sheep got into trouble, they lost a lot."

"Would that be the winter the lady left?" I asked.

"Lets see. Yes it would have been. Why?"

137

"Oh, I just wondered."

"Has this decision you say you have to make, to do with her?"

"In a way," I said vaguely

"How long do you intend staying?"

"Not much longer I don't think."

"Haven't you any friends you could talk to about your problem, your decision?" she asked.

"Oh it'll sort itself out," I said smiling. "In any case if I don't leave soon you may give me a paint brush."

"No maybe about it, it has to be done soon, before the season, or it'll never get done. Well, I must get on and wash the dishes and make some pasties and quiche for tomorrow." Eileen picked up her cup and saucer. "Do you want anything to eat later, you may get hungry?"

"Thanks, I will take whatever you have handy."

"Well, I have cheese and onion pasties, or scotch pies, or I could make you a sandwich. Afraid such a large group at this time of year caught me out, not got much left, there may be a little soup."

"Two pasties will be fine. Who knows I may even make some chips."

"And then again, you may not," was the response.

As Eileen packed my order I went to the toilet and caught a glimpse of myself in the mirror; my hair was now a long unmanageable tangle and my sweater was stained. There were dark grey patches under my eyes, and deep ruts between them. I looked a wreck and couldn't believe I had ventured out in such a state.

Chapter Forty

Back at the bothy, I looked at the papers on the table, paced around, sat down, got up immediately and put some water on to boil; then went to the window and walked away. What was I to do? All I did know was that I was very tired, mentally and physically; so laid down on the mattress; unable to settle, got up, made a drink and sat in front of the fire. What was I doing here? I was happy when I arrived and now I was in a hopeless state. Yet I knew the answers to all my questions, and if I couldn't find the peace I yearned for, neither could I ever forget my quest to find it; and if I couldn't then what was left? All that remained was to live in inescapable misery, and that was not an option. There was only one exit and Avylis had even closed the door to that.

Outside a mist was rising rapidly and within seconds had completely obliterated the landscape; a harbinger of doom I thought looking out at the grey wall that enveloped and entombed me. Was this the life awaiting me? Had my search for Avylis ended here, in a grey windowless cell with no door? Had Avylis faced this scene; these feelings; this torment? I knew she had. At the table I shuffled through the pile of papers that I had discarded either as repetitions or irrelevant.

> I was quite calm as I sat down to write to my friend, closing my eyes to concentrate. Without warning a 'thought', as clear as if spoken came,
> "I'm not listening."
> I opened my eyes; my mind was numb. Then I spoke.
> "If you aren't listening, then who is?"

There are no words to describe my feelings; for dread, fear, terror would not fit; the closest maybe would be abandoned. "If you're not listening, then who will? Who am I to talk to? There is no one else. What is the point of my life; what am I to do, as without you there is no point in doing anything. You were the only reason that made any sense for living or dying. I know that you are still there, I do not doubt that, but why have you abandoned me?"
But I knew my words had fallen on deaf ears.

~ ~ ~

Alone, plucked from familiar surroundings and dropped onto an alien barren landscape where survival was impossible; for here my mind, unable to understand, would desert me, unable to survive in a mist constructed of thick impervious stones, enclosing me in an icy, dark, airless environment without even a cleft through which hope may creep.

Having denied, betrayed and doubted that which I had known, in turn ignoring it, and taking it for granted, in the belief there would always be time; but even time had forsaken me. No use now feeling bereft. Forgiveness and companionship had fled, taking the gift of love that had nurtured me and on which I learned to trust implicitly; but I had failed to respond, and had thrown the gift back.

I had tried half-heartedly, but always retreated when asked to reciprocate it, at once stubborn and then apathetic, content to live as a child in its warmth and security; but a child, once secure and weaned has to grow, and I had refused.

Yet, how was I supposed to learn with nobody to teach me? My idea of love seemed alien in this world. All too late I'd learned I should have followed that which I inherently knew, and now it was too late. I looked, unseeing, at the mist that entrapped me, now that my friend had picked up the gift and left.

If Avylis had faced this, how had she survived? For it could prove nothing less than an intolerable torment, peace could never result from this. I could see her picture, deep - seated in my brain; the serene eyes, and yet the weather-beaten skin, deeply rutted with strain and torment, was that the result of living through this? It was definitely the result of something unimaginable…some sort of torture. And was it coincidence that her picture had been taken down? Maybe, or had she deserted me too? Don't be foolish, I thought, it had to be taken down. Nevertheless, it couldn't have been timelier. I was shivering.

Struggling to pull some firelighters out of the packet and putting them in the grate, followed by kindling and logs, I lit them, crouched close to the flames and poured hot water into a mug holding it unsteadily in both hands, as it spilt over the rim, but my hands were too cold for the nerves to transmit the inevitable pain, which was sure to follow.

"I've tried to understand her friend, Mick, or at least thought I had. Now I know all I had done was listen to others, believed others, instead of determining for myself; and in doing so had learned little and knew less, and had suffered trying to believe and understand all I had been told. I'm doomed, Mick," I moaned, "I have been here all this time attempting to avoid the decision; the decision, either to ignore Avylis, and live in comfortable misery, (which I had refused to admit was despair), or to believe in what I had read, and hope; that had been the stark reality; and I'd ignored it.

I did know her friend, or thought I did, but to me he was only an acquaintance, I had heard stories about, but those stories had only been interpretations and beliefs of others, and I had never doubted to begin with. When I did query them there was no-one to answer my queries; for everyone I consulted insisted they were correct; a few listened, but they didn't understand, and insisted that their beliefs were founded on ancient writings which couldn't be questioned; and shouldn't be questioned for to do so would surely lead you into desperation from which there was no escape."

I convinced myself that Mick was listening as he sat silently. "In that case Mick," I questioned, "how can her friend, who loved *her* unconditionally demand so much of others, and why are those others afraid and so sad?"

I went to the window, in the vain hope of seeing something, anything. An attempt to clear the ice from the window only left me with painfully cold fingers, but had no effect on the darkness now infiltrating the mist. I knew beyond my sepulchre were glorious radiant colours; a clear sparkling river, snow-capped mountains, that somewhere there was a sun and birds winging on their way in a clear blue sky, but they were in a far distant place now, gone forever.

How had Avylis escaped...or had her friend rescued her?

Just waiting and hoping was not an option, this darkness was impenetrable, there was no escape. Were those 'others' right after all? But even now in the inky darkness of my thoughts, I still couldn't believe that; for I knew and believed they couldn't be.

Struggling to keep my footing, I leaned against the wall, but I wasn't shivering as a result of the external elements, I was shaking uncontrollably from inner fear, sucking in rapid shallow breaths, I felt nauseous and faint. In...out, in...out.

~ ~ ~

The pain in my arm was intolerable; my face was screwed up with pain, as I tried to move my arm from under my body, the pain was excruciating. A thunderstorm was crashing about in my head, as I shook uncontrollably, causing every nerve and fibre to respond like electric shocks constantly running around my body. I was shackled, unable to move, and moaned, "Somebody help me. Please, somebody help me."

I rolled to one side to release my arm. Slowly the pain receded. Where was I? My hand touched the stone floor, I looked round at the inky blackness; then blinked several times, rubbed my eyes, lifted my hand and pulled an eyelid up.

"I'm blind!" Exhausted, I sobbed.

Memory returned. I needed a light, but didn't have one. "Think!" I crawled across the floor by the mattress, through the gap, felt under the slop stone, pulled the camping stove out, searched with my numb fingers, and using both hands managed to turn the ignition switch and the flame jumped up.

I crawled across the floor nudging the stove with the precious flame in front of me to the fireplace. My marrow was frozen. Unable to manipulate the box of firelighters I tore off one edge with my teeth and put the remainder of the packet in the grate, lit the piece of cardboard from the stove and threw it on the box, adding a log. Using the low chair by the fire I managed to pull myself onto it and then stand upright. Unsteadily I took the lamp down and splashed some oil in it, spilling most on the floor, and then left it on the table, now at *least* I had light, and could heat some water for a drink.

I stood by the window, wrapped in my sleeping bag, my mind in tatters. What was that? A light? I rubbed the window and stared; elated for a second, but it was just another tear in the fabric of my mind; I was hallucinating.

"I'm sorry, so sorry, but please don't torture me anymore," I pleaded, "I can't take anymore." I sobbed and rubbed the window again.

The amorphous light gradually strengthened as it passed, then disappeared. I continued to look at where it had been in despair, no longer able to trust my own senses. There it was again. A brighter light I had never seen, and I gazed at it in wonder as it dimmed, grew brighter, was obliterated, only to reappear. Now I knew! I looked at the moon gliding across the sky, through the cascade of pure joy falling down my face. The moonlight had pierced through my tomb "Thank you, thank you, thank you," I repeated until dawn, when the moon shared the galaxy with the rising sun.

~ ~ ~

"You hungry, Mick?" I asked, then remembered I had no food, so went to get some more oil for the lamp and saw the carrier bag on the slop stone and remembered the food Eileen had given me earlier; was that only today or yesterday, when? "Hey, Mick, we have a feast here."

It was ten minutes past seven. Piling the fire high with wood and coal, and with food and a cup of hot water, I crawled into my sleeping bag and with a hot water bottle on my knees, sat by the fire, ate until satisfied, and finally stopped shaking.

"Mick," I questioned, "How foolish have I been?" I avoided eye contact, not convinced he may actually tell me, but hearing nothing, I looked at him. Afterwards I watched until dawn gave way to a glorious sunny morning, and then finally slept.

Chapter Forty-One

I'd blinked at the sun, then got up immediately, lit the fire, filled the cauldron, and dressed. After feeding the birds I chopped the remaining wood up then had a drink; there was nothing left to eat, it didn't matter. When I had gathered my washing together including the sheet I had taken off the mattress on my arrival, I cleaned my little shelter thoroughly, looked at the results of my work, and satisfied, went to the car.

~ ~ ~

"I'm sorry but we are full," the lady at the Y.H.A. informed me. "But maybe if you could come back at about three?" she said glancing across at her colleague, who nodded. "It should be OK if you're quick, but we must give our guests priority, and we shouldn't really allow it, you know." I told them I understood, thanked them and left.

The nearby mobile café was still open, and after a mug of tea and packet of biscuits, set off along the riverside walk, before returning to the Y.H.A.

Leaving the hostel, I was once again reminded that they could not let me use their facilities again; it didn't matter. Thanking the lady and leaving a generous donation, I stepped outside into brilliant sunshine under a clear blue canopy and inhaled the clean air deeply.

As I headed back to the bothy elated, I waved to everyone I passed; I loved the world and the world loved me. The past weeks woes had rolled off my shoulders now my decision had been made, but first it was time to celebrate and I pulled in at the 'Malt Bottle' for dinner.

The young man, not a hair out of place, albeit a different style, in his immaculate uniform greeted me and relieved me of my anorak, as he said, "On your own today, madam?"

"Afraid so." I smiled as he asked if the table he indicated was satisfactory.

"You've changed your hair style, it suits you. You must have a good hairdresser," I said. The young man gave me a wide grin.

"My girlfriend has her own salon," he said, seating me at the table.

Has she now, I thought, guessing that the young man was no more than seventeen, and when he smiled looked even younger. It was simply a reminder of my own age.

Having decided that there was no point in self-restraint, having already demolished a roast chicken meal, when the waiter returned I ordered a Tia Maria coffee and sat contentedly.

The indecision and denial that had blinded me had been lifted, and while I was under no illusions concerning my future, I was happier than I had been for days, weeks; indeed had I ever felt quite like this before? I felt secure strong and happy, and yes... peaceful.

Driving back through the village I saw Eileen on the step of the now closed café waving at me to stop.

"You've got a visitor. He's staying at 'The Lamb', do you know where it is?" she called across. I nodded. "He asked if you could meet him there for breakfast at nine, tomorrow.

"Thanks." I said.

There was no point in reading any more of the papers, but reluctant to just put them back into the case haphazardly, I considered what to do. Many of them were very similar, repetitions, and these I had discarded in a pile of their own, after selecting a few relevant ones that drew them all together. The discarded ones I placed at the bottom, and then put the 'reporters' pads in. Finally, the papers which had proved relevant, I placed on top. It was like breaking up a jig-saw, leaving it a little easier for the next person to re- assemble, not that there would be a 'next person', I was just reluctant to leave something that had taken pains to sort out in an untidy mess.

The only paper left on the table now was the last I had read, crumpled, tear stained and unreadable. I picked it up; it was stuck to another, which I carefully separated, to find there were two more, too difficult to read, or were they? For on first discovering the papers, all to my eyes had been difficult to read, and why leave two, after reading all the others. I may as well finish the job, if it were possible.

Why do you fight me? Your hurt is mine do you not see that?
But you my friend were losing sight of me. That hurts.
Oh, can't you see, to lose someone you love so much, to be taken for granted, ignored, misunderstood; it hurts.
The pain you suffered, multiply it a hundred fold and more;
No my child you could not bear it; but I did out of love for you. You have only just begun to realise just what you ask of me, and I will refuse you nothing; but you also know I will not burden you.
Will you walk a little further with me, one step, and one day at a time... please?

"Please! He asks 'please! After all I've done – not done – broke his heart, and yet he *begs* me to let him continue to love me. Not only that but he promises that all I have to do is allow him!"

I had begun loudly in disbelief of what I was reading, but my voice quieted to a whisper, "You will *still* do that for me?" I continued to read:

This is all I ask of you. I will walk at your pace if you will but come. Will you trust me to do that?

He was like a teacher – no, he was my teacher – who patiently repeated the same lessons without giving any indication of impatience, frustration or despair, his only desire that his student succeeded.

"Yes." I whispered, and picked up the last sheet.

Self, others, time and place engulf;
Determining all.
Needs, wants, doubts and grief;
Invade on all sides,
Demanding urgent attention;
Refusing to be ignored.
The fight against the intolerable invasion;
The ill equipped soldier against the army;
Refusing to surrender.
Afraid to face his unknown fate.
Living with the impossible;
Awaiting the inevitable.

He falls; alone in the dark silence,
Senses forfeited;
Time and place forgotten.
Self and others are no more.
All that is left is
Breath as he sleeps.

He is woken by a whisper.
"Rise and follow me."
He trusts,
Reaches out his hand
Stands and goes;
In the knowledge that he can defeat the enemy,
In the silence of trust, love and forgiveness.
For he has learned to listen.

For the first time, now denial had been evicted, I not only understood but accepted what I was reading.

There was nothing left to do except sit by the warmth of the fire, all was in order for tomorrow. As for my visitor, speculation was futile; no one knew I was here.

Chapter Forty-Two

I had set the fire but not lit it; splashed cold water on my face, as an excuse for a wash, and dressed, before putting put my few belongings in the car Pulling the tartan rug on the mattress straight and replacing the sheet over it, I rolled the blanket up and placed it on the case. Finally I folded the few clothes and left them at the foot of the mattress, replacing the paper I had found back in the pocket. Just as I had finished, Mick ran onto the precisely made bed. Taking a deep breath, I exhaled silently, and slowly reached out my hand to stroke Mick with one finger, then gently picked him up.

"What would I have done without you? If I leave the rest of your choc for you, promise not to make yourself sick?"

Checking that my vehicle documentation and cash were safe in my money pouch, I placed it round my neck; and, after one last look round the bothy, I fixed the new padlock on the door and left.

It was not quite half past seven, and I steeled myself for the next half hour.

~ ~ ~

Ignoring the notice 'Closed' the door opened and I entered. Seconds later Eileen appeared.

"You're an early bird. Everything OK?" She asked as she made drinks.

"Fine." I said.

"What can I do for you so early?" she said placing two coffees on the table and sitting down.

"I'm leaving today." My smile was weak and my eyes smarted. Eileen was apparently at a loss for words, so I continued, "I've come to thank you for feeding me so well, and for your care and concern."

Eileen looked at me, sipped her coffee. "Where are you off to?" she asked.

"I don't know."

"I could be wrong," she sighed, "and if I didn't know differently, I'd think you were crazy."

"Maybe I am."

"Reached a decision then?" she asked.

"Yes."

"Well, I wish you well. Will you be back?" she paused, "I know, you don't know."

"Maybe, but I admit it's doubtful."

"Well you must do what you think best and I hope it works out for you."

"Oh, I'm sure it will." I said with a certainty.

Eileen raised her eyebrows, but remained silent, then changed the subject. "Have you seen your visitor?"

"Not yet, going now."

"Can I get you some breakfast before you leave? she asked

"No thanks, I'm supposed to be there by nine."

"Any idea who he is?"

"Not a clue, nobody knows I'm here. Did he tell you his name?" I enquired.

"No, and I didn't ask," she said getting up, "Well I'll go and make you a lunch box up - before I open - to see you on your way."

Eileen handed me the biscuit box, which had held a selection of twenty-four different assorted biscuits and had a snow scene on it, as I stood to leave.

"I really am very grateful. What I would have done without you? I should really have gone to thank the others but to be honest I'm not very good at 'good-byes'," I said, my eyes now wet with tears.

Eileen assured me she would relay my thoughts to the villagers and hugged me as I sniffed, and suggested that I washed my face before leaving.

"We'll miss you," Eileen said, "but I know the others would wish you well, wherever you may end up."

"Thanks," I sniffed, wiping the tears away with a tissue.

"Now you be off, otherwise you're going to miss your visitor and your breakfast."

"And you would never forgive me for missing my breakfast, would you!" I said with a half hearted laugh.

"Be off with you, and don't forget to send us all a postcard. I'll miss you, I'm sure we all will." Her voice trailed off to cracked note.

Chapter Forty-Three

I arrived at 'The Lamb' a few minutes early. It felt strange, this is where my stay had begun and here it would end. I wandered into reception a few minutes before nine. The man looking out of the window turned, his anxious features relaxed a little as he looked at me uncertainly. I walked towards him and as we shook hands his features melted into a broad smile.

"Good to see you again," Mr. Hodgson said. "Would you like breakfast?" I nodded enthusiastically, still lost for words.

He escorted me into the dining room where he pulled out a chair for me, before seating himself opposite and handing me the menu.

"I can't deny it's good to see you, but what brings you here?" I asked, "have you found another excuse, for playing truant from the office?" I asked, smiling.

"Not exactly, I am a man of leisure. I retired three weeks ago," he informed me. "There is just one matter outstanding however, which, if possible, I would like to resolve." He held my gaze, but I remained silent, remembering our first meeting.

"Where are you staying?" he enquired.

"At the bothy."

"You've been staying there, in the middle of winter?" disbelief on his face, "all these weeks?"

"Yes."

"But, David, my friend who secured it, said it was nothing more than a small tumbledown building in the middle of nowhere," he exclaimed.

"Well, he was right; but it also peaceful and the scenery is free

153

and natural, with nothing to mar the panoramic view, not so much as a telegraph pole, and no traffic. You can hear the stars twinkle and the dew form," I said.

"Do you mind telling me what has kept you here so long?" he asked.

Taken by surprise at the question, I thought for a minute.

"Curiosity, I wanted to try and find out a little about Avylis."

"And did you?"

"Enough to know it wasn't her I was looking for," I said

"Oh, how did you reach that conclusion?"

"Partly with the help of the villagers, but mainly by papers she left in the bothy, and her picture."

We were interrupted by the waiter.

"Papers?" queried Mr. Hodgson.

"Yes, quite a few, in fact a case full. To be honest if I had paid more attention to them in the first place I probably would have been long gone. As it is I'm leaving today."

"Do you mind me asking what was in the papers?" he asked.

"That all depends on the reader, Mr. Hodgson..."

"Oh, do please call me Bill, it reminds me I'm actually a free man," he informed me, and it would certainly make my task all the easier if he was relaxed.

"Well, Bill," It sounded very strange, but I had little doubt it was really William, "what I can tell you is that there was not one iota of identification amongst them."

He didn't pursue his enquiry, instead he picked up his cutlery and cut through a slice of bacon, and I followed suit.

Placing his cutlery neatly on his empty plate, and reaching for his cup he asked what I intended doing with the bothy.

"Just leave it," I said.

"Will you be back?"

"I doubt it," I said, taking a sip of my coffee

"Where are you off to?"

I'd already had this conversation once today. "I don't know, and it doesn't really matter. Not now."

Mr. Hodgson picked up his napkin and wiped his lips.

"You've changed you know," he remarked. "You look slimmer, hair longer but..." he trailed off, and then restarted, "you could renovate the bothy and stay there, "he suggested.

"The bothy and Avylis have both played their parts, no reason to hang onto them. Time to move on."

Mr. Hodgson, elbows on the table, chin resting on clasped hands looked directly at me. "I couldn't fathom you on our first meeting, and I've got to admit I'm still struggling," he confessed.

Pushing my empty plate to one side and my coffee to the other, I leaned forward. "You know Bill, not only are you a gentleman, you are professional and loyal to a fault. I would go so far as to trust you with my life."

He acknowledged this remark by raising an eyebrow with his smile, saying nothing, so I went on. "You've always known the background of Avylis, maybe not all, but enough, and you undertook your duty towards her to the letter, as a diligent solicitor. But you weren't acting in that role were you, this was a personal agreement, am I right?" There was no response, not so much as a blink. "You undertook to comply with her wishes, as a friend, nothing more?" His eyes looked steadily into mine as I went on, "You obviously had complete trust in each other. How that trust was forged is not relevant, for I too have come to trust you both implicitly. Ridiculous you may think, having only met you twice and Avylis in papers and a picture, but there we are. How am I doing so far?"

I received confirmation, with an almost imperceptible nod from him, his eyes remained locked onto mine, until the waiter, responding to my semaphore, came over and refilled my coffee cup, Bill covered his. Without warning, Bill's gentle voice rose several decibels as he declared, leaning back in his chair,

"You have *no idea* how pleased I am to see you!"

He immediately glanced round sheepishly at the other diners, but what I was certain would have caused him embarrassment at any other time, wasn't apparent, as he grinned like a mischievous schoolboy.

What on earth was going on? The solicitor had behaved

professionally to a fault last time we had met, and it had been obvious he was a gentleman of the old school.

He cleared his throat, sipped his coffee, and looked at me, "I came to inform you that there was a codicil to the will, which, I can now divulge, that is now I have met with you again."

I waited. "The bothy is legally yours that is not disputed. However, there is also land."

"What has that to do with me?"

"What I am trying to tell you is that Avylis didn't just leave you the bothy, but the land as well."

Struggling to understand this information, I watched the waiter as he filled my coffee cup, and recalled something.

"The bothy belonged to Avylis, but the farmland surrounding it didn't," I said relating the story Mrs. Bea had told me regarding the day I met Owen.

Mr. Hodgson, regarded me with admiration. "You certainly did your research thoroughly, but I'm afraid the story is not quite true. On free lease, yes, to help the farmer over hard times, but on the understanding it would be released either on the death of the farmer, or on the death of Avylis, back to her estate. This was a requirement insisted on by the farmer, not Avylis, but she conceded to it."

"That would explain why the farmer could never sell it to his sons."

"Indeed," he said.

"How did it come to Avylis?" Silence. Forget that one I thought. "There was an *awful*, and I use the word appropriately, trust in these long term plans, anything could have gone wrong,"

"True," he nodded

"How did you know she'd died? Did she carry any ID?"

"Not exactly. She had an S.O.S. you know, a 'medical alert'"

I nodded. "Was it was round her neck, on a piece of string?" I asked remembering her picture.

"Not sure about the string, but yes," he confirmed.

"That's the last thing I thought she would have had. She always seemed to want to be anonymous."

"Oh, indeed, but it didn't have the usual information in, just an address to be contacted."

"And that was yours?" I asked.

"Yes"

"Relatives?"

"None known."

"And her funeral?"

"According to her wishes."

"Of course." I said. We looked at each other. I knew that there was no point in asking further questions; I was certain that Mr. Hodgson had divulged all he was going to; but not all he knew. It didn't matter. We sipped our coffee in silence.

I watched the general activity of the restaurant for several minutes, before turning back to Mr. Hodgson.

Tell me Mr. Hod...Bill, what would have happened if I'd already left and you hadn't met me today?"

"They would revert to me."

"So, if I could not be found, the bothy and land would revert to you?

"Yes."

"Well then, the land and bothy are yours," I said without hesitation.

"I have to inform you," he said, "that the land is, or could easily be returned to prime farming land, or sold... and I've worked out the likely purchase price for you which, is substantial. I would urge you to consider the matter further." His eyes pleaded with me not to be rash.

The waiter was looking towards us, and I smiled indicating my cup, and watched as he crossed the restaurant with the coffee pot, picking up the conversation with my companion.

"Let me present it this way," I began hesitantly. "When we first met you left me with a conundrum, which I chose to try and solve, with no clues whatsoever. What I now understand, to my benefit, is that if these details had been divulged then, I would have been the poorer for it; as it is I now have riches beyond my wildest dreams; but Avylis knew that I had to discover that for myself."

Mr. Hodgson smiled with obvious relief.

"Good, then that's settled. I have all the relevant details with me, and all the accompanying documentation, and I have tried to...."

"No. No. Bill, I don't need those," I protested. Mr. Hodgson's face was a picture of confusion.

"Why would Avylis burden me with land and monies when she had no use for them herself?" I asked, and smiled, Mr. Hodgson frowned, his bushy white eyebrows moved closer together as if in private consultation.

"Well in that case how do you propose we resolve the matter?"

"Avylis trusted you, and that trust was well founded, and likewise I trust you."

Our eyes held for several seconds, but I couldn't help laughing inwardly at the expression on the face across the table. The eyebrows had finished their debate, but the lips, try as they might could not quite form their usual smile; his eyes flicked about across the restaurant, looking for words.

"You refuse a small fortune, have nowhere to live, and do not even know where you will sleep tonight, and you're not in the least concerned?" He asked. Mr. Hodgson was either clearly bemused, or simply looked it; I had no way of knowing but hoped it was the latter.

"Well in that case how do you propose we resolve the matter?" he asked again. I turned my gaze to the window and finally decided on a solution, that just maybe ...then turned back to see Mr. Hodgson, meditating over his coffee, and began to explain my plan.

"Avylis had a number of assets, which she chose to convert into love, and freely gave away, helping others to realise that love is far more enduring than money," I paused, "please will you excuse me for a moment?" Returning with my notebook from the car, I sat down and flicked through the book, found the appropriate page and handed it to Mr. Hodgson, and watched him as he read:

Love can only be given with sincerity; how it is received is no longer in the hands of the giver, and it may well be abused; but that is irrelevant, for the power of love lies in the very act of its being given. Those who are aware of this truth cannot explain it, only live it.

He looked across the restaurant, deep in thought. I drank my coffee. When he turned back to me, he held my gaze for a minute.

"So what is your solution to the situation?" he asked me.

"I propose that Avylis would have wanted her assets, which I suspect she did not leave in their entirety to me," his amazed look provided the answer I wanted, "to be continued to be used as she had done. In short Mr... Bill, I believe she would have wanted her never decreasing assets of love to be used, not just left to increase in financial terms, she would never have approved of that."

He shook his head, had he understood?

"Ignore love and it will die a lonely death," I stopped before adding the crucial question, "Would you be prepared to manage Avylis's assets?"

He looked at me and I could not decide from his eyes whether he understood my proposition absolutely or if he had not understood a word.

Chapter Forty-Four

We were the only ones left in the dining area, and it was obvious that the tables were being set up for lunch. The waiter was clearing the table next to us and I quietly apologised for holding him up. He glanced at my companion, who was in deep thought, seemingly oblivious of his surroundings, and reassured me that there was no hurry, and asked if I would like more coffee?

"I never refuse a coffee."

"Now how did I know that," he said with a boyish mischievous smile that would have put the sun in shadow.

"I'm on a lone mission to save the coffee growers of the world," I explained. We both laughed quietly and turned as Mr. Hodgson moved.

"Can I treat you to lunch?" I asked my companion. Mr. Hodgson brought his mind back to the immediate and looked at me puzzled.

"Lunch?" he muttered as he looked at his watch with incredulity, as the waiter asked if he would like a menu. "If you don't mind, yes please," he replied, gently tapping his watch face. "Have we really been here three hours, nearly three and a half?" he asked me. I took a deep breath and released it with grateful thanks that he'd agreed to stay.

"Well it's one of the advantages of being retired, you'll get used to it given time." I responded.

"Yes, yes I suppose it is." He smiled and excused himself. I watched as he walked across the restaurant, passing the waiter who was heading towards me.

"Just *exactly* how much coffee do you drink?" he enquired as he replenished my cup, making no effort to disguise his flirtatious smile.

"Oh, coffee is a side line, tea is the driving force," I replied with sincerity.

"If I didn't have commitments I'd join the campaign tomorrow," he stated earnestly.

"Oh, don't be too enthusiastic. It's not as easy as you may think drinking coffee by the bucketful and tea by the tanker load" He laughed, his azure eyes twinkling, as I decided his blonde hair was natural.

"Still join tomorrow if I could."

"You shouldn't be so impulsive," I warned him, "it could end you up in trouble."

"Biting off more than I can chew, you mean."

"Very definitely." I tried to be serious but his mischievousness was infectious. We grinned at each other.

Chapter Forty-Five

We ate lunch in comfortable silence, watching the activity of passers-by, including a few stoic hikers, and the incoming diners. Our conversation so far, at least concerning the vital element, had been akin to playing chess, words replacing pieces; most of which now lay abandoned at the side of the board, but the kings still faced each other on the playing field.

The waiter came to clear the table, enquiring if we wanted deserts. We both declined.

"Will you be requiring the bucket or the tanker Madam?" he asked me seriously.

"Oh," I replied, "I may as well empty the bucket, start on the tanker tomorrow."

"Very well, Madam," he replied with a smile.

Mr. Hodgson raised his eyes as if to reassure himself that he hadn't been teleported to another place whilst perusing the wine list.

"And will you be requiring a drink, sir? Coffee?" Mr. Hodgson began to order, deciding on a wine, paused, and suddenly felt the need for a whisky, quickly explaining that it was not his usual habit at lunch time. As the waiter walked back across the restaurant with a jaunty air, I translated for Mr. Hodgson, grounding him back on planet earth; it wouldn't do for me to lose him to the aliens just yet.

"Do you think you would have liked Avylis?" he asked.

I looked up from my coffee; where did that come from I wondered?

"Yes, no doubt about that, though I have to admit," I said,

laughing, "at times I could have gladly throttled the pair of you."

"Tell me Bill, if I'd already left—"

Mr. Hodgson interrupted, "If you had, then the bothy would have remained yours, but the codicil would not have been effected"

"Take heart then," I began again, "if you had not found me still here, you would have had to deal with it. What would you have done then?"

"I really do not know."

"No, of course you don't," I began gently, "because you were determined to do all in your power to fulfill Avylis's wishes. You went to a great deal of trouble to track me down, and also to explain about the codicil, and indeed obviously came prepared to hand over the assets to me today, if you could find me. No one could have faulted you for being unable to find me in the first place, say after a year; indeed no one could have faulted you if you hadn't tried at all. How did you track me down?"

"With great difficulty," he said with feeling, and I felt like a child being admonished.

"All I had to assist me was the fact that you *maybe* on the Scottish Isles in the winter time, *any one* of them."

"Not a lot to go on," I agreed.

"Especially when you apparently booked your crossings no more than a day in advance and *never* booked a return passage, *not even* an onward journey."

Goodness, I thought, suppressing a smile, Mr. Hodgson is becoming quite excited; but having successfully kept my serious expression, I said, "Sorry, but I ..."

"Please, explanations are not required. I am just so pleased you didn't hop off from here before I saw you again. You have no idea how pleased I am to see you."

"Thank you. I wouldn't have wished to cause you further problems," I paused, "The truth is...er Bill, whether you believe it or not, I believe that Avylis knew I'd refuse, and therefore had the reassurance that you would be left in control of her assets, and they couldn't be in safer hands. Can I ask you a personal question?"

"Yes."

"Have you any plans for your retirement?"

He looked up smiling and was instantly animated. "Oh, yes." His reply was definite. "I have always wanted to travel, see more of the country. I enjoy the scenery and often thought, even more so since my last two visits, of settling in Scotland, maybe on one of the islands. I have little patience now with the hustle and bustle of life, and my job has changed so radically over the past years. I felt restrained by so many factors, no longer free to help people as I believed they deserved." He glanced across the restaurant and back to me. "Once the house is sold I plan to buy a camper van to travel at leisure and..." his eyes now focused over my shoulder, his voice barely audible, "and find my very own Shangri - La."

Which would be?" I asked quietly.

His eyes remained fixed – I suspected on nothing – as he spoke. "Peace and quiet, and maybe...just maybe..." His eyes questioned me as he asked, "Am I being, naïve?"

"Not at all, except if you long for 'peace and quiet' maybe you would wish to reverse your priorities." I could almost hear Mr. Hodgson's mind whirring round on well-greased axles behind intelligent eyes.

"Quiet and peace?" he said, and thought again. "Yes, yes, I believe that is so, one can't find peace without first finding the quietness." He looked at me as he held his own inner debate.

"Quietness is relatively easy to find, at least for a time, as it depends on external factors, but maybe peace is that which you find within the internal quietness," he said and glanced through the window, then turned back and asked, "You said that it wasn't Avylis you were looking for, so what were you looking for?"

"Her friend. You see she didn't travel alone." I replied.

"Did you find him..., or her?" he enquired.

"Yes, I was already acquainted with him, but Avylis *knew* him, and led me through the barrier separating knowledge from true understanding."

We sat in silence for several minutes.

I was suddenly aware of someone speaking and looked up, to

face Mr. Hodgson.

You didn't hear a word of that did you?" he asked me, smiling.

"I'm sorry..."

"Pity," he said, "you missed a compliment."

"What? I did? Don't get many of those these days."

"I was just saying that you are a very shrewd lady," he smiled.

While I thought how to reply, he continued his observation.

"You've thought it all through haven't you?" he continued as I watched his smiling face.

"You knew didn't you?.

"Knew? Oh, yes, well you did provide me quite a few clues," I answered.

"I did?"

"You did indeed. When we first met, you had travelled the length of the country to see me. Solicitors must have various means and ways of tracking people down, which I suspected you'd hadn't utilised. Also, I doubted that *any* solicitor would have gone to so much trouble; they would have held the assets on ice, in case anyone turned up later. You gave me no details whatsoever, whereas you must have held some information on your client. Today you knew I had nowhere to live. I didn't tell you that. And lastly you readily agreed with me that Avylis would not have wanted her assets to be ignored."

"You're a very - what's that word the Scots' use - 'canny', that's it a 'canny' lady," Mr. Hodgson was enjoying himself.

"But you're not going to divulge anything else, and to be honest, if I was in your position, neither would I"

He watched me, as if trying to read my mind, or consulting his own maybe.

"I couldn't divulge details on our first visit..."

"I understand completely and..."

"Do you want to know?" he asked.

I found myself thinking Mr. Hodgson had passed the decision over to me. Did I want to know? I'd thought I did. Thought it was necessary, but why? I had learned everything that mattered. Avylis had left me the bothy, led me to her friend, and changed my life, as she had others; wasn't that enough? Wouldn't anymore be an intrusion into her life; a life that had offered me so much; knowing so little about me. Someone, who preferred to remain anonymous by choice. No, to ask personal details would be a violation of the love she had given me.

"No." I replied.

"I can tell you one thing which I think may help."

I didn't want to know! my mind screamed at me, horrified at what I might be about to hear, but unable to find words.

"I can reassure you, it is not directly concerning Avylis." Apprehension still stiffened my shoulders as I waited.

"You asked me if I would be prepared to manage Avylis's assets."

Relieved, I nodded.

"Well," he began, "Yes I will."

It was as simple as that. I had my answer.

I remained silent while he pondered on this for a few minutes, until he looked at me.

"Do you mind if I go and look at the bothy, maybe stay there a day or two?"

"I wouldn't mind in the least, but I think you're forgetting something."

"Oh?"

"It is yours." I handed over the small key, explaining, "I've left it exactly as I found it." Standing, I was about to shake hands, but suddenly found myself being hugged, and didn't know which of us was the more surprised.

"You are an exceptional gentleman, Mr. Hodgson, and I am indebted to you for your loyalty to Avylis, and for your diligence. Good Bye Mr. Hodgson and I wish you a long happy retirement, and you will find your 'Shangri - La,' I can promise you that."

"Thank you," he responded as he hugged me again. Over his shoulder I saw the waiters face with a look of... 'What's he got that I haven't!' I winked at him and walked towards the door, then half turned to glance back. Mr Hodgson was still on his feet watching me as I said, "If you bump into Mick..."

"Mick?"

"A field mouse. He prefers chocolate to cheese."

I left, wondering if Mr. Hodgson's right eyebrow would ever find its way back home.

Epilogue

The inspiration which facilitated my journey began with the unqualified love and acceptance which my mother imparted to me.

After her physical passing I felt lost and then discovered in an unexpected moment the source of that love and inspiration.

From this I learned that this powerful force does not originate from any individual but comes from the limitations of our humanity.

The beauty is that any of us who are prepared to participate in the life of that force – anyone of us – may in turn creatively impart it to others.

About the Author

Sylvia was born in Salford and educated in Manchester. She has always had a desire to travel so after training in nursing, (SRN, RSCN & S.C.M.) she travelled overseas and worked primarily with children with Government Agencies and private organisations in Zambia, Aden, Saudi Arabia and Iran and in 1980 worked with Save the Children in Uganda.

Sylvia has written throughout her life and in 1970 the seed of this book was sown as she used writing as a channel during a particularly difficult period of her life. Latterly Sylvia writes for pleasure and in 2000 she undertook some formal studies in creative writing.

The Silent Mentor has been written over a seven-year period.

Sylvia continues her journey and now spends most of her time wild camping in the Highlands and Islands of Scotland where she feels most comfortable and at ease...

Lightning Source UK Ltd.
Milton Keynes UK
UKOW040606220312

189378UK00002B/3/P